ATTACHMENT-BASED MILIEUS FOR HEALING CHILD AND ADOLESCENT DEVELOPMENTAL TRAUMA

of related interest

Therapeutic Residential Care for Children and Youth
Developing Evidence-Based International Practice
Edited by James K. Whittaker, Jorge F. del Valle and Lisa Holmes
Foreword by Robbie Gilligan
ISBN 978 1 84905 792 9
eISBN 978 0 85700 833 6

Attachment, Trauma, and Healing
Understanding and Treating Attachment Disorder
in Children, Families and Adults
Terry M. Levy and Michael Orlans
Foreword by Sumiko Tanaka Hennessy
ISBN 978 1 84905 888 9
eISBN 978 0 85700 597 7

Therapeutic Residential Care for Children and Young People
An Attachment and Trauma-Informed Model for Practice
Susan Barton, Rudy Gonzalez and Patrick Tomlinson
ISBN 978 1 84905 255 9
eISBN 978 0 85700 538 0

Children and Adolescents in Trauma
Creative Therapeutic Approaches
Edited by Chris Nicholson, Michael Irwin and Kedar Nath Dwivedi
ISBN 978 1 84310 437 7
eISBN 978 0 85700 356 0

ATTACHMENT-BASED
MILIEUS
FOR HEALING CHILD
AND ADOLESCENT
DEVELOPMENTAL TRAUMA

A Relational Approach for Use in Settings from
Inpatient Psychiatry to Special Education Classrooms

JOHN STEWART

Foreword by Dan Hughes

Jessica Kingsley *Publishers*
London and Philadelphia

First published in 2018
by Jessica Kingsley Publishers
73 Collier Street
London N1 9BE, UK
and
400 Market Street, Suite 400
Philadelphia, PA 19106, USA

www.jkp.com

Library of Congress Cataloging in Publication Data
Names: Stewart, John Neal, 1954- author.
Title: Attachment-based treatment milieus for children and adolescents :
   healing trauma through caring, consistency and connection / John Stewart.
Description: London ; Philadelphia : Jessica Kingsley Publishers, 2017.
Identifiers: LCCN 2017023159 | ISBN 9781785927904
Subjects: LCSH: Attachment disorder in children--Treatment. | Attachment
   disorder--Treatment. | Attachment behavior in children. | Attachment
   behavior.
Classification: LCC RJ507.A77 S74 2017 | DDC 618.9285/88--dc23 LC record
available at https://lccn.loc.gov/2017023159

British Library Cataloguing in Publication Data
A CIP catalog record for this book is available from the British Library

ISBN 978 1 78592 790 4
eISBN 978 1 78450 739 8

Printed and bound in Great Britain

Dedicated to
Colin, Amanda and Nola

A young family whose spirit and love for one another endures
and sustains through the most complicated of journeys

APPRECIATIONS

To my wife Jan, the love of my life, a friend like no other and, from what I am told, a very patient woman.

To my kids and their families (Sam, Dana, Ava and Anna, Joey, Crew and Willa), who have brought me more joy and pride than they will ever know.

To my Mom, Dad, Brother and Sister, who have always been supportive and completely welcoming.

To Dan Hughes, from whom I have learned so much concerning attachment and who gave so generously in his support to me in writing this book.

To Lou Cozolino, whose books have been an inspiration and whose kind support in the reading and writing of this text served to keep me at it.

To my good friends in Portland and Seattle who help me not take myself too seriously.

To my many colleagues who have made this work an endeavor in life-long learning and fun.

To the children and families I have served in my practice and the day treatment program who have placed their trust in my care and taught me so much.

To Rachel Avery, my colleague, long-time friend, a great source of support to my writing and the provider of excellent feedback as a reader.

To Colin Lamb, a very good young psychiatrist, supportive reader in the writing process and most appreciatively my friend.

CONTENTS

FOREWORD

Dan Hughes

If they are to develop well, young people (kids and teens) need relationships with caring adults who are committed to them. Such relationships enable the structure and functions of the young person's brain to become robust and organized. As the brain flourishes it exerts its influence on the development of all areas of the body, including the physiological, sensory, emotional, social and cognitive systems. Through such relationships, the young person is able to attain their developmental milestones ("act their age") and pursue a path that is ideally suited for their interests and skills, hopes and dreams. The type of relationships that best meet the needs of young people are known as attachment relationships. (Other relationship systems in the brain are those of companionship and of hierarchy. These are secondary to attachment in their role in human development.) Attachment relationships are based on providing the young person with a sense of safety through being available, sensitive and responsive to him or her. For the adult to be considered to be "sensitive and responsive", the adult needs to join with the young person—to connect with him or her—moment to moment within attuned interactions, synchronized to the initiatives and responses of each, as well as joining with them in their personal journey where they develop the skills that lead to meaning and purpose in attaining their lifetime goals.

Young people who live in psychiatric hospitals, residential facilities, group homes, or day treatment and specialized educational programs that focus on acute and severe behavioral problems tend to be those who have not had the opportunity to engage in attachment relationships to provide them with experiences that they need for their development.

Very often the adults responsible for providing them with consistent care did not do so for many reasons. Less often the young person was not able to respond to good care due to past experiences of relational trauma or to constitutional reasons. If these young people are to respond to the various programs designed to address their acute and severe behavioral challenges and to assist them in developing their various skills, these programs need to be centered on providing them with the relationships that they either never had, or, when they were presented to them, were not trusted and so were rejected.

Young people who were traumatized by relationships or the lack of relationships need healthy relationships to heal, develop in an integrative manner, and some day thrive. There is more evidence for the need for a strong therapeutic relationship if treatment is to be successful, than for any other therapeutic quality. Two recent issues of the American Psychological Association journal, *Psychotherapy*, focused entirely on the necessity of the therapeutic relationship for success in all models of psychotherapy as well as on the characteristics of such a relationship that are "evidence-based" (Hilsenroth 2011a, b). The contributors conclude that a central component of training programs for any model of psychotherapy must involve training in understanding and developing the therapeutic relationship (Norcross and Wampold 2011).

Yet, developing such relationships with young people who do not trust relationships is often very difficult. Our natural ways of creating safety and engaging others in meaningful relationships often fail with these young people, and these failures may create insecurities, doubts, shame, anxiety and anger in the adults who are trying to "help" them. The young people are not likely to trust the motives of the helping person, especially when they are being told "no" about something that they want or when limits are set on their behavior. The young people often lack the skills needed to engage with others in a reciprocal manner, to cooperate, communicate or regulate the emotions associated with the interaction. They are also likely to have difficulty resolving conflicts and engaging in relationship repair. These challenges for the young person create corresponding challenges for the adult. Being consistently rejected by a young person for whom the adult is offering care primes that adult for entering into a neurobiological state of "blocked care" (Hughes and Baylin 2012). Adults in that state do their job in caring for the child, but they have lost their heart in the process, and the young person is certain to experience the adult's disengagement from the interaction and be less likely to risk trusting that person. Also, adults, entering into a relationship with a young person who is being encouraged to form an attachment with them, are likely to have their own attachment history experiences activated. If there are any unresolved issues or themes in their attachment histories, these are likely to emerge and make it very difficult for the adult to remain engaged with the young person in a manner that is in their best interest.

Another area of difficulty for the adult attempting to provide safety and trust for the mistrusting child involves the adult's need to experience relational safety themselves with the other adults involved in the young person's care. The relationships among the adults, whether focusing on the relationship between the manager/supervisor and the front-life person, or the relationships among the front line staff, need to demonstrate an open-and-engaged attitude, where they experience mutual support and where conflicts are able to be addressed and resolved. In family therapy, the need to attend to the relationship between the couple when there is a challenging child is understood as being necessary if we are to assist the child to experience safety and improve his or her functioning. The same attention needs to be given to the relationships among the adults in residential or day programs for young people who do not trust relationships.

Given these significant challenges to developing safe, healing, and transforming relationships for young people who find relationships to be very difficult, it is tempting to focus on technique and skills to teach the adults who then are to teach the young people how to inhibit, regulate and choose their behaviors. The focus moves then toward the external structure, evaluations and consequences, as well as cognitive and behavioral coping skills, which will, hopefully, enable the young person to change their behaviors and move from failure to success, problems to strengths. We tend to forget that any such interventions are likely to be much more successful if the young person has an open-and-engaged relationship with the adult, in which they trust their motives, and are interested in their guidance and support. We also tend to forget that forming these relationships is often very difficult (Baylin and Hughes 2016).

We do have a great amount of knowledge available to us in the literature of attachment, trauma, intersubjectivity, early child development, neurobiological research, as well as research on the therapeutic relationship–knowledge that will guide us toward developing relationships with young people who have been hurt in relationships and now need to learn to trust relationships. Going with the young person into his inner life and developing with him a safe relationship is a more complex task than developing a program involving acceptable behaviors and teaching skills and providing a structure with consequences to attain our goals. Such structure, limit setting and cognitive-behavioral goals are of value. But, we need to begin at the beginning. An infant is defined in the infant-mother bond. A young person is defined within the context of the safe and trustworthy relationship where she or he is able to grow.

John Stewart's new work, *Attachment-Based Milieus for Healing Child and Adolescent Developmental Trauma*, is an excellent endeavor to describe the complex qualities that are central in developing and maintaining a milieu that provides young people with the relationships that they need to begin to trust and proceed with their development. Dr. Stewart provides a strong theoretical framework—based on our latest knowledge in the literature mentioned above—for understanding and developing a corresponding day-to-day program based on that theory. The principles are comprehensive in addressing all relevant areas of the young person's development. The interventions are consistent with the theory, while being teachable, and often quite creative. Dr. Stewart gives many examples of events and challenges that will be recognized by professionals in this field while also providing excellent examples of moment-to-moment ways of communication and engagement that will often successfully address them. Finally, Dr. Stewart gives attention to the adult relationships within the programs, and the challenges that providing care to mistrustful young people creates in these relationships. This work broadens our focus beyond the individual relationship that the adult has with the young person to all of the relationships within the program.

John Stewart makes it clear that providing services for young people who have acute and/or severe behavioral challenges, and who do not trust the adults providing these services, is a very difficult task. But a very important, meaningful and satisfying one when we are able to make a difference in the lives of these young people. It is important for us to remember that, though our task might be very difficult, the challenges that these young people have faced are likely to have been much more difficult—and most likely will continue to be—unless we are able to help them to learn to trust us and take advantage of our compassionate care and our competent guidance.

References

Baylin, J. and Hughes, D. (2016). *The Neurobiology of Attachment-Focused Therapy*. New York, NY: W.W. Norton.

Hilsenroth, M. (ed.) (2011a) 'Special issue: Evidence-based psychotherapy relationships.' *Psychotherapy 48*,1.

Hilsenroth, M. (ed.) (2011b) 'Special issue: Evidence-based psychotherapy relationships II.' *Psychotherapy 48*, 4.

Norcross, J.C. and Wampold B.E. (2011) 'Evidence based therapy relationships: Research conclusions and clinical practices.' *Psychotherapy 48*, 98–102.

Hughes, D. and Baylin, J. (2012) *Brain-Based Parenting: The Neuroscience of Caregiving for Healthy Attachment*. New York, NY: W.W. Norton.

PREFACE

A professional life straddling the domains of mental health and education has afforded me much opportunity to observe our institutional attitudes and approaches to understanding and addressing the needs of our most complex children. My work across these disciplines has been associated with helping a child struggling within a system (e.g. treatment program, special education classroom, daycare, peer group, family) through changing the child to fit the system, the system to fit the child, or more often than not, both. In reflecting on my many years of clinical work, I fear that too often I have become fascinated by the analysis of the child's psychosocial and neurocognitive profile, not focusing enough on their core and normative need to "feel felt," accepted, lovable and loved. It is in response to this reflection, along with the exploding volume of neuroscience research suggesting the same, that the book that follows is written.

The use of the word "love" in discussing "clinical work" evokes a wide range of responses. While none will openly speak out against the importance or power of love, bringing this highly personal construct into the clinical domain creates considerable anxiety for many.

In asserting the role of love in effective child clinical work, a variety of responses will typically follow, ranging from, "Yes, of course, behind all of this clinical jargon what a struggling child needs is competent loving care," while others react with, "Well yes of course they need love, but what they really need is structure and predictability," and perhaps others with, "Of course love is great, but it is accountability that has been lacking in these children's lives; this is what is needed to allow them to grow."

The good news in addressing these seemingly disparate perspectives lies in the fact that "competent loving care" demands structure, predictability and accountability all delivered with loving kindness in a stable (attachment) relationship.

The enormous explosion in neuroscience research supporting the centrality of attachment to growth and development is largely associated with the increased availability of neuroimaging techniques. This technology has allowed the neuroscientists to work alongside developmental psychologists in mapping the function and needs of our ever-evolving brains, resulting in study after study showing connection with others as fundamental to our evolution and individual adaptive capacities.

This research has fueled a convergence in the fields of human development and psychology unlike at any other point in my lifetime. The eloquent work of those such as John Bowlby, Daniel Stern, Dan Hughes, Alan Schore, Louis Cozolino, Dan Siegel, Guy Diamond, Bruce Perry and Mary Gordon, to mention a few, have brought these research findings into meaningful understandings to inform our thinking and approach to children. At the core of what is being offered by these evolving insights is the fact that emotionally attuned connection is both the pathway to optimal development and the road back from aberrant development.

In my work with clinical populations within schools, I have often encountered wonderfully compassionate and creative teachers and school-based mental health staff working tirelessly to find the "magic" that will allow their students to be competent and effective learners. Too often, though, I have watched these same teachers moved to tears, anger, powerlessness and hopelessness as they struggle with a difficult student; a situation often driven by their obligation to *teach, teach, teach*, while operating in an institution that has limited awareness of the imperative to first support the child in feeling connected, cared for, respected and perhaps in some core sense loved and then to teach.

As their psychological consultant, I understood my role as that of supporting teachers in understanding their student's behavioral and learning issues; a process that has too often taken the form of offering a label for the child's struggles (i.e. ADHD, autism, and so on) and inadequate encouragement to connect and perhaps courageously love this child. This is not to suggest that a coherent and compassionately offered diagnostic understanding of a child cannot be helpful in promoting attuned and supportive connection; however, should this clinical understanding create within others a sense that the child's needs are beyond their capacity to fully understand or meet, it is rare that this sense will not prove to be the case.

If a psychological understanding of a child is to be helpful it must serve to increase empathic attunement, provide a clearer sense of the child's needs and hopefulness in the caretaker's capacity to meet these needs. In the absence of any of these three out comes a psychological model for understanding a child is of little utility and may even prove detrimental.

Early in my career I had several opportunities to consult with small island schools off the coast of Maine. When called to these schools to address the needs of a difficult student, my review of the child's record invariably revealed the profile of an extremely troubled youngster with complex history, behavior and needs. In approaching these consultations, I was often struck by how different they felt from consultations with mental health and special education settings on the mainland. In time I grew to recognize that the not so subtle difference was associated with the island teachers' sense of ownership of the child. These teachers demonstrated virtually no ambivalence concerning their obligation to the child: difficult or not, they were theirs. These island teachers operated from a level of commitment that seemed to offer a wonderful capacity to take consultation recommendations and implement them with positive outcomes often not seen on the mainland. What I grew to understand, and even more so now, is that what these teachers and their students had was geography that left them little opportunity but to attach. No specialist would sweep in and take over the child's care/instruction; no one was going anywhere, leaving the teacher a deep *parent-like, loving* obligation to give this child what they needed. Invariably, this seemed to mean loving this child first and teaching them second.

It is not my intent to idealize these "island teachers" for I believe they were normal teachers placed in extraordinary situations that demanded of them profound ownership of their students. In a culture such as ours, characterized by transience and impermanence, an adult who comes into a child's life with the attitude that "you are mine and I am yours" has great healing potential for troubled children. As we consider what supports our children in both developing well and/or healing, the role of a deeply committed and attuned caretaker[1] (e.g. parent, grandparent, teacher, therapist) able to tolerate feelings of powerlessness, overcome hopelessness and remain emotionally connected to a challenging child cannot be overstated.

Bruce Perry, a renowned child *traumatologist* (a mental health researcher/clinician specializing in work with trauma victims), credits as one of his most powerful teachers an elderly foster mother by the name of "Mama P." Mama P, who is described as a large African American woman from the inner city with a lengthy history of effectively fostering troubled children, had as her credo "What my babies need is love!" (Perry and Szalavitz 2006).

This is in no way to suggest that "loving these babies" is easy, for more often than not struggling children are profoundly ambivalent about "being loved," both desperately wanting it and terrified to put themselves in the vulnerable position of trusting and needing another when not feeling worthy of such loving care. Over time, in response to inadequate caretaking these children develop a self-narrative of, "I am bad, unlovable and can trust no one." A challenge to this painful self-protective identity is almost always rejected until tested repeatedly. A child's testing of a caretaker who is offering a distinct reflection of the child is often unconscious, albeit profound and diverse—much like our approach to a frozen pond in early winter, particularly if having fallen through the ice in the past; a troubled child challenges the strength of the ice at the edge of the pond, stomping with increasing force until convinced of the ice's strength. It is only after such results that they can invest in a willingness to move to the deeper area and greater risk. For those either naïve or courageous enough to be the *ice*, hold on; the ride will be anything but easy or smooth; however, the payoff, when successful, is extraordinary as the child shifts away from defensive self-doubt into believing themselves lovable.

As the connection between a clinician or clinical caretaker and a difficult child begins to evolve, the maintenance of this emotional bond must be safeguarded. This does not mean doing only as the child wishes (or demands), freedom from behavioral limits, or protection

---

1   Throughout this text the term "caretaker" is used in a generic sense to describe anyone in the position to care for a child, including but not limited to: parents, foster-parents, older siblings, extended family, teachers, therapists and even law enforcement personnel.

from behavioral consequences. What it does mean is fulfilling these obligations with connection and kindness.

Similar to driving on a slippery road, the relational connection (traction) between a struggling child and a clinical caretaker must be the primary focus. In the absence of traction (connection), pressing on the accelerator will result in little progress, while pressing harder even less. This being the case, the clinical provider who knows how to maintain connection while navigating a difficult relational road involving limits and consequences possesses the skill set for the clinician and child to both "arrive safely" at a destination of healing.

In my frequent role as a clinical consultant to public schools, it is not uncommon that in reviewing the record of a chronically struggling child I will discover a prior year in which the child's adaptive functioning was greatly improved, only to be followed by renewed difficulties in the following year. More often than not, as I have tried to understand this variance I discover a child and teacher who seemed to have had a close relationship: a student who says things such as, "Ms. Smith was different, she really liked me and thought I was smart," and a teacher who reflects with such comments as, "I don't know why, I just really loved that kid." These teachers invariably report some of the same difficulties as others, but regardless hold the child within a warm and loving place in their memory. This kind of "loving mirror" seems to play an important part in the child's experience of something wonderfully different within themselves, and in doing so manifests this more positive sense of self in improved functioning across the domain of behavior and academics.

How powerful it is for an adult to love a child in a manner that affords them hope of being lovable, particularly when the child's behavior does not make this easy.

With my primary professional identity on the mental health side of the disciplines I straddle (education and mental health), I would so love to be able to say that it is my perception that we clinicians uniformly share a deep understanding of the role of relational connection (attachment) in development and healing. Sadly, however, this is not the case. But this is not to suggest that those within my field are not adequately kind, caring and compassionate; rather, it is to say that associated with a wide range of factors, perhaps most importantly our own relational histories, as a field we have dramatically under-attuned to issues of attachment.

In place of a focus on core relational issues such as the child's sense of being safe, cared for and perhaps most importantly loved, much of the mental health community's focus has been on the development of coping strategies and behavioral shaping through contingencies and medication intervention. This is not to suggest that there is no value in these interventions, but it is to assert that should these strategies be applied outside of, or in place of, a caring and connected relationship, it is much like carefully filling a water bucket when the bucket has a large hole in the bottom.

As will be described in this text, some of the imperatives for attachment-informed work fly directly in the face of accepted behavior-shaping techniques such as concern regarding a child's achievement of "secondary gains," the practice of "planned ignoring" and the idea of placing a highly dysregulated child to some form of isolation (from "time-out" to "quiet rooms") until they are able to regulate their emotions.

Sadly, from an attachment-informed perspective too much of what is done with dysregulated children (most often the ones with complicated attachment histories) to "help them learn to regulate emotion and behavior" is guided by the frustration and hopelessness that can accompany work with these children. Often in the name of structure, accountability and consequences, even we mental health providers resort to a "bigger hammer" in the management of the child's behavior. This hammer can take the form of bigger consequences (e.g. you can't live at home until you behave, you can't leave the unit until you behave) and bigger enforcers involving teams of adults ready to uphold the limit to the point of escorting a child to seclusion, and powerful doctors drawing a line in the sand and walking away. A model of intervention that is unintentionally, yet nonetheless far more coercive than therapeutic, often serves to recreate the very dynamics that underlie the child's pathway to aberrant development.

These coercive expressions of frustration, together with a heavy reliance on a social learning model (belief that all behavior is learned and shaped by positive and negative consequences) direct too much of our work with troubled children serving to limit attachment sensitivity. It is only in the context of unconditional acceptance and attunement to the child's available capacities that behavioral feedback and consequences are useful. In much the same way we approach infants, we cannot get lost in efforts at upholding "accountability" for a capacity a child has yet to develop, a capacity that will only develop in the context of attachment.

Unfortunately, coercion, whether done in a clinical context, by a parent or malevolent dictator, **can** effectively quell a good deal of difficult behavior, yet at a price marked by increased anxiety, a more damaged self-narrative and reduced trust in the interpersonal world. The distinction between a situation in which a kind and wise adult provides a child important and useful structure, containment and consequences, and one in which the adult provides detrimental coercion is almost fully tied to the emotional availability and support of the adult to the child in the process. When a caretaker can set a necessary limit or deliver a consequence, while simultaneously remaining emotionally attuned and supportive, the limit is useful and healing. When a difficult limit is set and the child is left to manage painful, perhaps even unmanageable emotions on their own, little is accomplished in supporting capacity for emotional regulation, or the child's core and fundamental belief in themselves as lovable and therefore safe in the care of others.

This assessment of our clinical endeavor is in no way meant to villainize the many hard-working and committed mental health providers working tirelessly to help the kids in their care. It is, however, my desire to say that as a field, particularly when serving in the role of a clinical caretaker in settings such as psychiatric hospitals, day treatment programs and special education classrooms, we must strongly strive for our relational stance to reflect what science is teaching us about our kids' needs. We must be open to a pathway for clinical intervention that is less focused on the expedient changing of behavior and more focused upon healing the injured hearts of the children we serve. The text that follows endeavors to provide milieu-based clinicians with attachment-informed insights and strategies to promote healing (perhaps even loving) emotional connections within the clinical setting.

INTRODUCTION

A world such as ours, characterized by an extraordinary rate of cultural change, can have a broad and profound impact on child development. Perhaps the most critical effect is the stress that this instability places on the family, undermining its central role in enculturation and the provision of a platform from which the child develops a core sense of self and an associated sense of self in relationship with others.

In an effort to understand the changing nature and role of family, it is helpful to recognize that up until the last century our species practiced a parenting style referred to as *alloparenting*; a practice in which a range of family members play an active role in a child's parenting. This practice allowed multiple caretaker–child attachments as a child's needs for attuned love and care were the concern of a range of family/tribe members. At the turn of the last century the average number of family members actively and lovingly involved in a child's care was seven; however, contemporary research drops this number to under two. This shift suggests that more and more of our children's caretaking needs may be falling between the cracks, as they go unnoticed and/or are addressed by less attuned non-family, paid or institutional figures with whom the child may enjoy limited emotional connection or attunement.

Coincidental with this shift in our child caretaking patterns, our culture has experienced a large and problematic jump in the percentage of children and adolescents exhibiting challenging emotional and behavioral development. When considered together with contemporary neuroscience research, which emphasizes the absolutely critical role of relational connection to virtually all aspects of child development, this coincidence demands our attention. Should we understand the increasing number of struggling children as linked to relational issues endemic to the culture's changing pattern of child caretaking, it is imperative that we pursue both primary and secondary interventions. Primary intervention would occur through the provision of better family supports (i.e. longer maternity/paternity leave for new parents, better and more flexible daycare, safe and secure housing, parent mentoring, and so on) and in providing training to institutional caretakers in emotionally attuned secondary care intervention, entailing clinically informed efforts at corrective relational experiences for children suffering the impact of poorly attuned caretaking.

This text was written to support mental health clinicians working within treatment milieus in the development of *parent-like*, or more scientifically "attachment-informed," relational stances. Unfortunately, connecting with and meeting the needs of children who have become relationally disenfranchised and believe themselves unlovable is generally far more difficult than doing so with more typical children. Nonetheless, the basic tasks involved with both populations are essentially the same, similar to skiing down a beginner slope, vs. a double black diamond: the technique is fundamentally the same, but the challenges in balance, speed, edge control and management of apprehension are far greater on the steeper hill. If able to ski down the easier slope, however, with desire, practice, patience and courage you can in time master the advanced slope. The basics in skiing do not change greatly between more gradual and steeper trails, nor do the basics of relational connection between typical and clinical populations, yet the challenges in exercising these basics with the struggling child are far greater.

The model presented in this text focuses on the importance of understanding and responding to children's social and emotional needs as the pathway to both positive psychological development and healing. The fact that the vast majority of children and adolescents with significant emotional and behavioral difficulties have histories of problematic, under-attuned caretaking and/or relational trauma (physical, emotional or sexual) demands the restructuring of their relational experience. The majority of these children have suffered under-attuned care and/or abuse by parents who have loved them, but simply do not have the mental health, or empathic, intellectual or financial resources to **consistently** understand and meet their needs. A smaller but still significant portion of children have had traumatic experiences from which their attuned and competent parents have not been able to protect them (e.g. serious illness, loss of a parent, pre-adoption trauma), and neurocognitive compromises that frequently place them in situations that they experience as overwhelming (e.g. autism, schizophrenia, ADHD).

For those working within non-clinical settings, the majority of the children encountered have had more or less adequate relational experiences and will comfortably project these experiences onto non-parental caretakers. For these children, each positive encounter supports the expectation of future positive experiences and a propensity to view others in a positive light. A negative relational experience for these children is far more likely to be attributed to factors much less destructive than a core sense of being "not good enough" or even worse, "unlovable."

For the increasing number of children with significantly problematic caretaking histories, however, their relational self-narrative and relational expectations become pervasively negative. As this occurs, the child experiences an increased activation of lower-brain defenses, such as decreased flexibility, compromised learning, limited capacity for emotional regulation and problematic behavior. For this group of children, research shows that their chronically dysregulated brains impact learning in a manner that drops them approximately five years behind their peers in academic learning for each year of school. For these students, each failed or unsuccessful experience increases the expectation for future failure and moves their central nervous system further and further towards a chronic state of readiness for peril, dysregulation and further impaired learning. Each experience with an adult who misjudges their capacities and either under-, or over-challenges them (see the section on optimal frustration in Chapter 5) results in the child's decreased capacity to trust and rely upon themselves or their caretakers. Unfortunately, this inability on the caretaker's part to ensure a sense of attunement (feeling felt) and safety and the provision of support in discovering an evolving sense of competency undermines the child's ability, or willingness, to honor and trust in authority.

When a child has experienced his caretakers as incompetent (misattuned), metaphorically over and over again driving the car in which he is a passenger off the road and into a tree, he becomes compelled to habitually grab the steering wheel (take control) as an act of self-preservation. Unfortunately, this lack of faith in one's caretakers is rapidly generalized, resulting in a compulsion to "grab the wheel" regardless of the driver's competency. Taking the metaphor one step further, as the child grabs the wheel from the competent driver (i.e. his nurse, mental health clinician, teacher, and so on), perilously veering them off the road, it serves to affirm the child's negative expectations and profoundly impacts his relationship with his caretaker. The caretaker now experiences the child as *a problem* and a trigger for anxiety, undermining her capacity for the attuned intimacy and connection needed to shift the child's relational expectations and heal. This metaphor captures a cycle that tragically plays out over and over again within these children's lives.

Too often our response to such children (as they grab the steering wheel) is the expression of strong disapproval, consequences and punishment. Unfortunately, this kind of response, although intuitively valid (*a negative consequence will reduce the likelihood that the behavior will be repeated*), with many children increases the likelihood of the behavior. This response often places child caretakers (both clinical and non-clinical) in the position of escalating consequences as they seek the "magic bullet" that will bring the child into more compliant behavior.

I cannot count the times that I have been called into a situation with a difficult child to hear a report of a series of ever more severe consequences that have been applied to attempt to change the child's behavior with no, or worsening, effect. Unfortunately, when the only model available to understand a child's difficult behavior prescribes the wrong intervention (punishment), we often seem locked into a pattern of prescribing larger and larger "doses."

The attachment model provides a very distinct way of understanding child behavior and dramatically distinct interventions. Unfortunately, selling this model to our culture will not be easy in that in many respects it is counterintuitive and thwarts the moral satisfaction of the *eye-for-an-eye* response. If our current model continues to fail as it is currently, desperation may turn us towards a more compassionate and wise management of those among us who are struggling. With such a shift it is to be hoped that the massive resources we direct towards punishment will be reallocated towards relational connection.

This noted, it is important to realize that even with newer and more attuned models for intervention, attachment is difficult and slow work requiring emotional attunement with children who initially are unwilling to accept it. This work that will activate frustration, powerlessness and anger within clinical caretakers as we put our best effort forward and often experience these children as cutting off any limb on which we climb out on their behalf.

Our objective is to convince these troubled kids to trust in us and to accept us as valid mirrors, reflecting to them a different story about who they are and what they can expect from others. It is the slow work of creating these healing experiences for troubled kids requiring tremendous commitment and compassion that allows them to change. This work requires as much as any the capacity to bring both our heads and hearts into our effort to support healing.

Conclusion

There is a great deal of evidence to support the argument that we have little choice but to embrace a different relational approach in our mental health treatment programs, particularly for those children with problematic relational histories. The increasing number of disaffected children within our culture affirms the "Why?" of this necessity for change, leaving us to address the bigger question of "How do we shift our relational approach in these critical institutions?" Fortunately, contemporary attachment and neuroscience research provides excellent counsel and guidelines for this work. Nonetheless, the implementation of these insights and guidelines is not a simple task for it is far easier to help a child along a positive relational path, than to pull them back from a negative one.

This endeavor often confronts us with the obligation to change the heads and hearts of our caretaking professionals, in order to change the heads and hearts of our children. In many cases we are asking these caretaking providers to make a fundamental shift in their caretaking paradigm and roles. This shift will be possible for some and not so for others. This change will be most difficult for those guided heavily by a contingency-based (social learning) model for interaction with a heavy focus on behavioral accountability and the power of consequences to bring a troubled child into line.

This is not to suggest that there is no role for mental health professionals who cannot make the leap to an attachment-informed model. There are caretakers who are gifted at scaffolding complicated learning to support children in an evolving sense of competency. As these individuals work with children and adolescents who have more positive caretaking histories that allow them to readily trust and not challenge their caretakers, a less emotionally attuned provider will not represent a significant problem. However, in work with younger and more vulnerable children and adolescents, a provider who does not work within a relational model is unlikely to be effective, and may serve to worsen the child's underlying relational mistrust and negative self-narrative.

Extensive research predicts that an individual's ability to work positively within an attachment-informed model is associated with their **understanding** of their own attachment history. Interestingly, the factor predictive of strong potential capacity to operate within this model is not an individual's attachment history but rather their understanding of their relational story. An adult could well have had a very difficult (poorly attuned, neglectful or abusive) relationship with their own caretakers, but if this individual has created a self-narrative that essentially says, "This was wrong and I did not deserve this treatment," they will be in a good position to help a struggling child to heal. Should an individual have a difficult caretaking history of poorly attuned, neglectful, coercive or abusive care, however, and not recognize it as such, or not realize that it was not their fault, their potential to interact with a struggling child in a healing manner is quite limited. In other words, it is not what has happened to us in the process of growing up that predicts our effectiveness with struggling children, but how we insightfully understand it. This ethereal variable is a critical prerequisite for effective work with our more complex children; however, it is extremely difficult to meld into administrative policy. In the final analysis, work with these children is highly personal and if we pretend that a staff member's relational history and narrative are not relevant to hiring and professional supervision, we fly in the face of sound judgment and research.

For all, perhaps particularly those who work more naturally within a relational model, the emotional challenge in connecting with a child who relentlessly rejects and tests every invitation to connect is slow, exhausting, frustrating and often accompanied by feelings of powerlessness. Nonetheless, **this is the only way forward** with these sad, angry and complicated kids; and for those who manage to stay in the game, ultimately connecting, there are few experiences more heartening or compelling.

As a point of departure in our effort to impact our clinical culture, I offer the following perspectives and recommendations, each discussed in more detail at later points within the book:

- Strategies for both the *prevention* and *healing* of issues of attachment are fundamentally the same, therefore the training needs for professionals working with clinical and non-clinical populations are largely the same.

- A core sense of physical and emotional safety on the part of the children and the staff serving them is essential to any program's clinical effectiveness.

- Positive and secure attachment and associated capacity for emotional regulation are critical to academic, social and emotional learning across age groups.

- Attachment-focused insights and values are most reliably expressed in the work of front-line staff if reflected throughout the institution; therefore training within an organization should always begin with the leadership team.

- *Attachment-informed* work within organizations is greatly facilitated when staff are managed in a manner sensitive to attachment dynamics. (*"It is difficult to treat the children with whom we work better than we treat one another."*)

- Initial training, ongoing support and a self-reflective relational stance are required if an attachment-informed approach is to be effectively and consistently provided.

INTRODUCTION TO THE ROLE OF TREATMENT AND THE TENETS OF ATTACHMENT THEORY

Some reading this text may choose to move directly to the later section on the application of attachment theory, feeling less interested in the *Why?* of this model than the *How?* This is certainly an acceptable option, yet for those interested, greater theoretical background can be helpful in supporting the creative application of the model. Similar to the adage *feed a man a fish and he will eat for a day, teach him to fish and he can eat for a lifetime*, a relatively clear understanding of the fundamental tenets of attachment theory can be extremely helpful in informing our thinking and manner of responding to the wide range of children, behaviors and situations we encounter in our effort to support thriving and healing.

Chapter 1

TREATMENT WITHIN A THEORETICAL MODEL

The text that follows has both the explicit goal of advocating for an *attachment-informed* model for use within intensive child and adolescent treatment programs, and an implicit objective of supporting the critical importance that such programs operate within a clearly articulated theoretical model; an objective tied to the belief that it is the theoretical model that defines both the desired destination (outcome) and a map for the journey (treatment approach). I hope that the reader will leave with an increased appreciation for both.

To many, perhaps even more so those outside of the mental health field not burdened by the trees obstructing the view of the forest, the idea that our most intensive child and adolescent treatment programs often work void of a clinical model is both remarkable and troubling. For those of us in the mental health field, the loss of an obligation to work within a clear clinical model had been a death by a thousand cuts, blinding us to the often rudderless nature of clinical work uninformed by a model. The truth is that we do not know what we don't know and that the decline of model-driven milieu-based clinical treatment has been so long and pernicious that many younger clinicians have never had experience with a program guided by a well-articulated and applied model.

At the core of a psychologically informed treatment model is the staff's shared understanding of the roots of maladaptation (mental illness) and the pathway and strategies to support healing. Work without such a model is much like a complicated journey without a map or compass. In some respects we are not even sure where it is that we hope to arrive, for as posited by Dan Siegel (2008), as a field we really do not have an agreed definition of *mental health*. This leaves us with a journey which we know intuitively to be incredibly important and profoundly challenging, yet on which we depart with a lack of clarity on our destination and relatively few aids to navigation.

This is in no way meant to demean the incredibly difficult and valiant work being done in our intensive treatment settings. These programs are often saving children's lives and doing so with great commitment and compassion. What I am saying is that these programs too often work without a well-articulated and applied clinical model allowing for optimally effective consistent and coherent intervention.

At present many intensive child and adolescent treatment milieus function largely in the role of providing safe containment, often supervised and managed by staff with relatively little training in mental health treatment and no real understanding that their program is operating without a core model and as such largely flying by the seat of its pants with nothing more than a *behavior management program* (which many confuse for a *treatment model*). Again, it is no one's fault that they do not know what they do not know; however, it is our responsibility to attempt to discover what we do not know, particularly when this knowledge might be critical to our very important goals and objectives.

Not to glorify the sometimes problematic earlier history of milieu-based programs guided by the psychoanalytic model (i.e. the work of A. Freud, M. Kline, F. Redl, B. Bettelheim and W.D. Winnicott), it is fair to say that the programs driven by this model had a coherency that supported their efficacy. They also enjoyed a relatively high level of staff satisfaction associated with cohesion in the staff's shared understanding of the work and their roles. Again, this is not an appeal to go back to the analytic model, but rather an appeal to go back to a coherently expressed and applied psychological model within our intensive treatment programs.

It is my belief that our loss of a need/obligation to work within a psychologically informed model is not associated with indifference on the part of the clinicians working within these programs. I believe it is a response to a wide range of factors and pressures including, as already noted, limited exposure to model-driven treatment programs during training; movement towards a biological model for mental illness; pressure to shorten and reduce the length and cost of intensive treatment and an associated reduction in resources for milieu development and supervision; the emergence of a heavy reliance on intuitively-based social learning approaches (reward and punishment); and the fragmentation of the field with each discipline (i.e. psychiatry, psychology, family therapy, occupational therapy, and so on) making its own contributions. All of these factors erode the likelihood for programs to have a unified treatment model to inform and guide their work.

The second purpose of this text is to outline and teach an attachment-informed treatment model, to offer a way of understanding why the children we serve have fallen off the path of normal development and what they need to find their way back onto the path. The fields of attachment and interpersonal neurobiology have exploded with new insights on development and mental health over the past 20 years, yet relatively little of this has made its way into the management of intensive treatment milieus. This model is intuitively sound, internally consistent and increasingly research supported.

As a clinician having developed and supervised intensive treatment milieus for almost 40 years, I have never been more hopeful and excited about what we now know concerning the roots of maladaptation and the pathway to healing for troubled kids. Yet at the same time I am profoundly discouraged by how little these insights inform many of our most intensive treatment programs.

It is my belief that the attachment-informed model offers us a wonderfully wise and compassionate way to work within intensive treatment milieus. This model has the potential to bring staff together to a clearer understanding of their roles and mission and to a greater sense of cohesion and associated work satisfaction. Most importantly, it provides a clear framework for both our treatment goals and the strategies that support healing. It is my deepest of hopes that this text is helpful to the reader in discovering the power of this model to understand those we serve, and support healing in these vulnerable children and adolescents.

This is the purpose of this text.

Chapter 2

WHAT ATTACHMENT THEORY TELLS US IS WRONG WITH THESE KIDS AND WHAT THEY NEED

Consistent with the message of the preceding chapter, we turn to our clinical model and a three-step process to answer the question, "What's wrong with the kids served in intensive treatment settings and what do they need to heal?" First, we rely on the model's representation of what is required for things to go well in the course of development; second, we use the model to develop a hypothesis concerning what did or did not happen to undermine the child's thriving; and third, we employ a method to address the hypothesized issue. Analogous to a problem with an automobile that will not start, first we consider the principal factors needed for the car to run (i.e. the car needs fuel and a charge from the battery to start the internal combustion cycle); second, we develop a hypothesis concerning which aspect of the needed variables might be lacking (i.e. the battery has no charge, or the car has no fuel); third, we address the hypothesized problem (i.e. we charge the battery or add gas). In our work with struggling kids the process is little different: We start with an understanding of what is needed for development to go well and from there identify what aspect of these needs has been missing and use this understanding to direct intervention.

In simple, yet still useful terms, what the attachment model tells us children need to thrive is a trusting sense of safety and security in their relationship with their caretakers and an evolving capacity to use their caretakers in the co-regulation of emotions, leading to the capacity for self-regulation. In light of this understanding we can generally conclude that *what is wrong with the kids we serve in intensive treatment settings* is broadly linked to limitations in each child's experiential background of one or both of these factors. Clearly, there are other issues that might be addressed in answering this question (e.g. neurocognitive and neurobiological factors), yet virtually all can be related back to functional limitations within these two spheres and experience that has thwarted this development.

In the context of attachment theory, these two core capacities to trust in the care of another and to regulate emotions are fully linked; for it is only in the experience of safe, attuned and competent caretaking that a child can allow a caretaker close enough to support them in the management (co-regulation) of their difficult emotions. This is not to suggest that supporting a child in learning to regulate their emotions requires nothing more than a safe and secure relationship with their caretakers, for as is described later in the text, this is a required but not sufficient factor in developing the capacity to regulate emotions.

The next chapters will provide an overview of attachment theory, starting with a discussion of what it means to be *attached* and how attachments serve us, then moving on to how attachments are formed. They will also discuss what can go wrong in the course of development from an attachment-informed perspective and what is needed in a treatment setting to allow a child to heal and thrive. In most respects the healing process prescribed entails the clinical milieu operating in a manner that emulates the positive–normative process of parenting, seeking always to promote within the child a sense of safety and trust in their caretakers and teaching the management of emotions through attuned co-regulation.

As we move into the discussion of an attachment-informed treatment milieu, it is important to understand that this model in no way supplants the need for a well-structured and predictable treatment environment. It does, however, greatly emphasize the fact that if it is to be healing, this structure must be upheld in a non-coercive, respectful, attuned and connected manner. The text will discuss the dimensions of this required structure, as well as insights and strategies for upholding structure and boundaries in a manner that promotes connection, emotional regulation, positive self-narratives, and a stable and secure sense of self. The text also presents a three-stage model for attachment and discussion of the nature of the relational needs at each stage, as well as attachment-informed work with special populations.

Chapter 3

INTRODUCTION TO ATTACHMENT THEORY

Over the last two decades our knowledge in the field of psychology and human development has undergone extraordinary growth, moving further and further from a simple contingency–social learning model organized around positive and negative consequences to explain and address behavior. The burgeoning fields of interpersonal neurobiology, attachment and traumatology have brought enormous advances to our understanding of the developmental needs of all children, as well as a far more sophisticated model for understanding and addressing the needs of those more complex and problematic children. At the core of our evolving understanding of child development is far greater insight concerning the role of relational connection, or *attachment*, in virtually every aspect of a child's growth and acquisition of adaptive capacities.

What is attachment?

Whether approached by the poet's heart and words or the scientist's thoughts and measurements, relational *attachment* cannot be described in a manner that is fully satisfying. As an aspect of human experience so dear and profound that virtually all roads of thought and feeling lead back to it, attachment is at the core of our humanity. Recognizing the breadth of this concept, we will limit our focus and lean in the direction of science, all the time realizing some things are not easily, or maybe even reasonably, subjected to scientific method and its demands for objective and quantifiable measurement.

Although attachment relationships can take many forms, our discussion will first center on normative positive or secure attachments in the child–caretaker/parent relationship, then move into more problematic forms of attachment. Attachment in this context will be defined as an adaptive, reciprocal, biological, cognitive, emotional and transcendent sense of connection, a connection characterized by deep feelings of belonging and empathy, an essential interpersonal bond involving our minds, brains, bodies and spirits.

Explained from a developmental perspective, attachment is that sense of belonging or connection that evolves as individuals interact with one another in a meaningful, attuned and empathic manner, providing a core sense of safety. This connection in adults has bidirectional aspects, but in the caretaker–child relationship it is organized around the child's experience and reliance upon the caretaker for safety. In the context of this safety the child is able to increasingly move towards comfort in the experience of "feeling felt" by the caretaker.

The experience of being positively attached to another translates into a sense of safety, trust and well-being when in their presence; and over time even when separated. Research has shown that the presence of someone to whom we are attached (an attachment figure) triggers the release of the soothing hormone oxytocin, as well as several neurotransmitters serving to quiet and soothe the central nervous system and optimize the polyvagal nerve (Stephen Porges, 2011); particularly the lower brain, which is so focused on safety and capable of overriding and incapacitating upper-brain functioning when activated by threat.

Attachment as a developmental variable is not as much a "trait" as a "state," in that even though one's relational history may set the stage for a tendency to approach relationships from a particular perspective, it does not mean that this approach is immutable or universal. Clearly, there are those with a greater proclivity for attachment than others largely based on the character of their relational history and temperament, but the character of one's attachment within an individual relationship is associated with the issue of *fit* between those individuals, not simple capacity of one or both. This fit is governed by a wide range of issues and becomes hugely important as we attempt to support those with negative relational histories in moving towards more positive and useful ways of functioning within relationships.

Within a developmental framework a *positive attachment* is a relational connection that allows for a sense of safety and security based on the belief in others and their capacity to understand and consistently support the meeting of one's needs.

Why are attachments important?

The discussion of the importance and function of relational attachment is an enormous topic, which if addressed fully would be well beyond the scope of our purpose. If asked in relatively simple terms, however, avoiding the broader (i.e. poetic and evolutionary) implications of attachment, we can say that relational attachment is critical to the development of the capacity for *emotional regulation* so essential for higher-level thinking and learning, in addition to providing a cognitive and emotional template to thrive within communal living.

Access to our higher cognitive capacities, housed in the upper brain or cortical region, is directly linked to our management or regulation of the lower brain's stress–threat response system. This is due to the fact that all sensory input passes through the lower brain (brainstem, diencephalon and limbic regions) to arrive in the upper brain (cortical region). Therefore in the presence of a highly reactive or agitated lower brain, sensory input does not efficiently reach the upper brain. This being the case, the lower brain's stress responses must be modulated if sensory information is to pass through up to the higher cortical region for more complex processing and learning (i.e. reasoning, abstract thought, understanding of self and others and academics).

The neurosciences teach us that the lower brain has an almost exclusive focus on self-protection regulating body functions (e.g. temperature, breathing, heartbeat), and monitoring and responding to basic issues of safety. We also know that the lower brain becomes conditioned by experience to be either predominantly quiet, or chronically activated and ready for potential threat. This conditioning of the lower brain by experience sets the stage for an infant or child fortunate enough to have a well-attuned caretaker who is able to keep them safe and meet their needs to have a lower brain that is generally quiet or regulated and able to pass information up through to higher regions of the brain for effective learning. This efficiency translates into more sophisticated adaptive patterns and learning. Research on the impact of lower-brain activation on school functioning has shown that children with chronically activated lower brains (dysregulated) fall as much as six months behind in academics for each year of schooling.

When a child is not stressed, the higher and lower regions of the brain are effectively integrated, in which case the whole brain is contributing to the open and engaged, reflective and affective manner of knowing and relating.

In further understanding the role of attachment in our development and functioning, it is necessary to recognize that the brain is "all about" associations, or the linking of one experience with another. This association process involves the brain's structural and chemical hooking up of neurons that have been fired simultaneously (e.g. when a young child is encountering the family pet the word "dog" is spoken by the caretaker, and over time when the word "dog" is said the child imagines the family pet). In time the firing of one neuron automatically leads to the firing of the other. As often stated in the neurosciences, "Neurons that fire together wire together."

Through early regular positive caretaking experiences the child forms an association between caregivers and a state of well-being. Therefore the "good mom" neurons that fire when she is present will later, even when she is simply remembered, activate the "I am safe and my needs will be met" neurons and the lower brain remains quiet. This association sets the stage for the child to be emotionally regulated and seeking of caretaker help or support when stressed by perceived peril or an unmet need. Each time the caretaker is able to effectively provide this support, the association between caretaker and well-being is strengthened and the child becomes a bit less prone to emotional or behavioral dysregulation under stress.

Early in development the child begins to recognize the caretaker's pattern of matching or reflecting their affective state prior to addressing a need. This may take the form of the caretaker's exaggerated facial expressions, as they smile back at a smiling infant, or make a sad face towards a child expressing distress. This pattern of matching the nature and to some extent the intensity of the child's emotional state prior to effectively addressing the child's need sets the stage for the child to associate "matched affect" with the meeting of a need. This "matching of affect" in the support of emotional soothing is often referred to as the first step in *co-regulation* of the child's emotions. This association translates into a process wherein the child's experience of an attuned caretaker, able to empathically reflect a matched affect, serves as a source of emotional soothing.

As a child grows from infancy to adulthood their capacity to move towards *self-regulation of emotion* increases through the process of managing an expanding range of emotions in a collaborative or *co-regulation process* with attuned others. This process of co-regulation must occur frequently if the child is to move towards the capacity for self-regulation. Those individuals in a child's life who care for them and effectively co-regulate emotion become important and powerful "attachment figures." Over time the child's association and connection with these attuned caretakers allows these relationships the power to soothe or support emotional regulation, not only when in the presence of the caretaker, but also through the child's thoughts and memories of this relationship.

Dan Siegel and Tina Bryson's (2012) simple but eloquent metaphor of the *river of well-being* is useful in understanding the adaptive responses of both clinical caretakers and the children they serve. In this metaphor Siegel and Bryson describe *adaptive well-being* as the caretaker and child being in the middle of a river marked by two banks, one characterized by chaos (e.g. tantruming, confusion) and the other rigidity (e.g. shutdown, inflexibility). Well-being, and perhaps *mental health*, is found in the middle of the river as we manage life's challenges without being pulled towards a bank or, as is too often the case, from one bank to the other.

There is great utility in knowing that both we and the children we serve are subject to drifting between the banks of chaos and rigidity. It is also important to recognize we have a tendency towards one bank or the other when under stress and accordingly to be self-aware to avoid this maladaptive drift when possible.

To understand both our own tendency to drift from the center of the river, as well as the tendencies of the children with whom we work, affords the clinical caretaker important insight. The attachment-informed model teaches that the most effective way to stay in the middle of the river, or to find our way back to the middle is through connection, metaphorically suggesting that it is only in connection with others that life challenges will not pull us away from the middle of the river and when need be that connection allows us to make our way back to the middle.

In answering the question, "What do attachments do for us?" from a psychological or developmental model, we can say they help us manage our emotions so that we can access and use our higher-level thinking and learning. In the absence of the capacity to regulate emotion, we remain ever on the verge of more primitive, less adaptive lower-brain responses (drifting towards the banks of the river) to perceived threats and unmet needs.

From a neurological perspective, it is important to understand that these early life experiences start *wiring our brains* for how we will experience and relate to others; do we approach others as safe and valued, do we experience and respond to empathy and in turn offer it to others? The power of these early experiences noted, it is also imperative that we recognize that in response to experience our brains continues to evolve and that the impact of earlier problematic relational experience can be mitigated by more positive or healing relationships.

Attachment is effectively at the core of our ability to be our best, most adaptive self alone and in community.

Chapter 4

ATTACHMENT NEEDS WITHIN A THREE-STAGE DEVELOPMENTAL FRAMEWORK

A basic understanding of the course of development with respect to attachment needs affords milieu-based caretakers a helpful framework to predict, understand and respond to the needs of the children they serve. A milieu guided by this insight is able to more effectively target children's needs, supporting development; and conversely, a milieu operating outside of this insight is likely to thwart or even reverse essential attachment development.

Not unlike a construction project to rehabilitate a damaged building, even if the more evident damage is seen in the upper portion of the structure, it is imperative to address problems within the foundation prior to attending to the region above, always working from structural issues below to the next level above. It is only in having a basic understanding of the developmental course of attachment that milieu-based caretakers will target foundational needs prior to those at a higher level. This fact is often not intuitive in that a child's chronological age frequently does not correspond to their developmental or emotional age, demanding of caretakers discernment between what the child *should need* at a given age and recalibrating to what they **do need**.

The developmental model presented offers three stages, each building on the previous one with the potential for developmental regression when under stress. This model is derived from my many years of observations within a K-12 day treatment program where I had served as Clinical Director for 25 years. Again, the stages are not dictated by chronological age, but rather a child's relational history; a child who has not experienced well-attuned care could remain at stage one into adolescence or even adulthood; whereas a child who has experienced himself as having been well cared for might show signs of stage three development as early as age three or four.

Many factors play into the child's subjective experience of the quality or nature of their caretaking, including such issues as their neurocognitive profile, medical history, life circumstances (e.g. poverty vs. affluence), temperament and temperament match with their caretaker. It is entirely possible that a caretaker could seem to have strong attunement and commitment to caring for a child from an objective perspective, yet variables such as their neurobiology (e.g. autism) or life circumstances (e.g. growing up in a war zone) negatively impact the child's subjective experience of this care.

It is also important to realize that a child's developmental stage is not always static across relationships. It could be that within some caretaker relationships they are functioning at a significantly higher or lower stage than in others. It is fair to say that children may well have a predominant stage of development from which they operate and that this is the stage from which they enter relationships, but it would not be useful to think of a child as functioning at the same level across all relationships. Those relationships that elicit a sense of attuned caretaking from a child will always be drawing the child forward in development and those in which the opposite is true will support developmental fixation or regression.

The three-stage model presented is similar in some respects to that offered by Erik Erikson in identifying developmental outcomes as dichotomous, wherein development at each stage is defined by a continuum: 1. *Safety and security* vs. *insecurity and shame*; 2. *Emotional regulation* vs. *emotional dysregulation*; and 3. *Meaning and purpose* vs. *meaninglessness*. Each of these developmental outcomes directly impacts the child at the level of core self. Each promotes an integrated and secure experience of self, or in the negative direction a more brittle and fragmented self. This is tied back to the fact that it is through *connections and reflections* with and from others that our core self most evolves.

Each stage is discussed here.

Safety and security vs. insecurity and shame

This initial stage of attachment development typically plays out during infancy and early childhood, a period in which the primary focus of the child's caretaker is on meeting basic needs for protection and sustenance (safety) and the provision of security associated with the caretaker's presence (physical and emotional). Should these needs not be subjectively experienced by the child as well met in early life, however, further development will demand their being met at a later point. The meeting of this need for a sense of safety and security in the context of connection with another at a later point in childhood, or even adulthood, remains possible, but more difficult and demanding of a far greater reliance on the symbolic experience of safety and security provided by another, as opposed to simple, direct caretaking. This symbolic offering of "safety" could involve the individual's experience of a caring, attuned and competent teacher, boss, therapist, landlord, platoon sergeant, grandmother...having a seemingly unconditional and largely effective commitment to supporting them in the obtainment of fundamental needs and relational attachment.

The experience of safety and security for a child is determined by their caretaker's ability to consistently understand and meet their needs while at the same time expressing pleasure or joy in this advancing emotional connection with the child. Unfortunately, in the absence of the caretaker's ability to routinely keep the child safe and to express joy in doing so, the child's core sense of safety and security will not be met. It is only in experiencing the caretaker as both competent in their care and joyful in its provision that both safety and security are promoted. In the relative absence of either of these variables, the child will not have the foundation for later stages of attachment development; and due to normal childhood egocentricity, will develop an understanding of what they did not receive as associated with their inadequacy. In others words, if my needs are met, *I feel lovable and worthy of good care and because I am lovable my caretaker is going to stay around and continue to meet my needs. If things do not go well and my needs are not met it is because I am unlovable, I bring limited joy to my caretaker and cannot count on them—all of which I feel shame for.*

In Kohut's (1971, p.116) words, "a child first learns who he is in the reflection of the mother's eyes." It is this positive, focused emotional affirmation (adoration) of the child that serves as the initial building block in both the child's sense of self and their sense of connection with others. In the language of the Velveteen Rabbit (Williams 2017), being loved is what makes us real, and in the absence of an adequate experience of such care and adoration we remain insecure and shameful for our being unlovable. Without the experience of safety and security there is no cohesive self. Instead, the experience of self is that of being no more than a fragmented collection of randomly organized thoughts, feelings and perceptions.

Sadly, there are many situations that can undermine a child's experience of *care and adoration*, ranging from parental depression, substance abuse, childhood trauma, mistreatment, painful and frightening medical procedures to highly vulnerable neurodevelopmental profiles (e.g. autism). These factors and others can result in children in dire need of corrective relational experiences affirming their worthiness of love and care.

The work within the treatment milieu is often foundational from an attachment development standpoint. Within the treatment program we must meet the child where they are developmentally, and if working with a child whose early caretaking needs have not been adequately met, then healing must begin with the attuned meeting of the child's basic needs for safety and nurturance and the expression of joy or pleasure in their provision. In the absence of this, limited further attachment development will occur.

This is a tall order for milieu-based caretakers! You take in children in dire need of loving and attuned care, who more often than not carry deep shame for not being who they needed to be to elicit good care and in this shame are unwilling to let us close; in the words of Dan Hughes (2007), setting the stage for the caretaker to face the challenge of blocked care to eliciting blocked caretaking. This is a very difficult dynamic demanding great wisdom and compassion from the caretakers of these children, a level of care that we can aspire to yet must be gentle with ourselves when unable to achieve. In many respects it is our ability to continue to show up, try our best, forgive, repair and do it all again tomorrow that allows for the healing to occur and this first stage of development to be achieved with kids who have had a tough start.

Examples of interactions that support a child in feeling safe and cared for joyfully

> » "I know you hate being here and you kind of hate all of us who work as staff, but I am just going to sit quietly with you because you deserve to have a grown-up not telling you what to do and just letting you know that you matter."

> » "I know you said you weren't hungry and didn't want anything I would offer, but you are a good kid who has had too much to deal with and I would feel so much better if I at least knew you weren't hungry on top of everything else."

> » "I know you get really mad at me, but even though you are upset and saying all kinds of hard things to me, I am so impressed by how creative you are—[smiling] you have called me some names I have never even heard before."

> » "I know you said you wanted to be left alone and I will try to do this, but I also know that you deserve to be cared for and taken care of, so I will just sit quietly outside your door and if I can help in anyway, let me know."

> » "You were doing so much spitting when you were angry and wanted us out of the room that I bet you are really dry. Can I get you some water?"

Later in this book Hughes's (2007) acronym PACE (playful, accepting, curious and empathic) is presented as the pathway to connection; when a child is blocking our care due to their lack of development at this initial stage there are few tools more helpful than those of the PACE model.

Emotional regulation vs. emotional dysregulation

The second stage of attachment plays out in a dichotomy defined by *emotional regulation* vs. *emotional dysregulation* and centers on the child's learning to manage difficult emotion through the co-experience and co-regulation of those powerful affects. As has been mentioned earlier, the two most common and related adaptive variables bringing children into intensive treatment are limitations in the capacity for safe and secure attachments (stage one development) and limitations in ability to regulate emotion (stage two development). This being the case, it is imperative that our treatment settings understand and address these issues if they are to be effective.

This second developmental variable clearly builds on the first, for should a child not feel fundamentally known and safe with a caretaker it is not likely that they will allow the caretaker close enough to support them when feeling vulnerable. Again in the language of Hughes (2007), a child who does not feel fundamentally safe with a caretaker will develop a pattern of "blocking their caretaker's care." On a fundamental level, this blocking entails not allowing the caretaker to meet basic needs, nor to support the child in managing difficult emotions (co-regulation).

The concept and approach to the critical developmental need for children to be supported through the co-regulation of their emotion is discussed in detail in a later chapter; however, for the purpose of understanding this as a developmental factor to be addressed in treatment, it is enough to recognize that children learn to self-regulate emotion only through having had many prior experiences of co-regulation of emotion with attuned and caring caretakers. This process entails an emotionally activated child (positively or negatively) as experiencing their caretaker as able to accurately reflect their affect; essentially joining them affectively in sharing their surface emotion but not their underlying dysregulated emotion and, once matched with the child, supporting them in quieting to a regulated state. The caretaker, as described by Daniel Stern, matching the vitality of the child's affect and then gently helping them calm, not unlike the wrapping of a blanket around a crying infant, being with his distress and letting your calm, calm the baby.

It is through this repeated process that children learn to develop a soothing trust in their capacity to quiet dysregulation allowing them to remain in their upper-thinking brains and able to accurately perceive, learn and respond to adaptive challenges. How difficult it is for someone, child or adult, to respond or adapt to a challenge when their higher-level thinking is short-circuited by a dysregulated lower brain. Few developmental capacities are more critical than learning to regulate our emotional reactions, and few developmental capacities are as dependent upon caretaker attunement and support than this ability.

Examples of interactions supporting co-regulation

> » A mom making a sad face as she approaches her baby who is crying and in a gentle and somewhat exaggerated manner saying, "Oh, little guy, what's the matter?"

> » A dad approaching a child who has just struck out at bat for the third time, with a gentle but somewhat sad expression, saying, "Oh, buddy, that stinks—I know how much you want to break this slump!"

> » A mom about to enter an amusement park with an excited three-year-old. Mom looking excited as well, says, "Oh boy, just think of the cool stuff we are going to do when we get inside! All right, how about you and I taking three deep breaths so when we get inside we are calm enough to really have fun, and following the park rules so we can stay here all afternoon? Ready? 1, 2, 3, breathe... Oh boy, I feel better and ready to go in, how about you?"

Meaning and purpose vs. meaninglessness

The last stage of our three-stage model focuses on the developmental need for a sense of *purpose and/or meaning* in the context of connection. This need seems to be associated with the relational security that comes from an experience of being useful or helpful to others. It is a need understood best in thinking about our evolution in the context of tribal life, where the security associated with feeling and believing that the tribe needs you as much as you need the tribe is profoundly assuring and comforting.

Those children fortunate enough to feel safe and adored, as well as confident in their capacity to regulate emotion (assuring access to higher-level adaptive capacities even in the face of a challenge), are able to move from self-preservation to concern for others. In making this shift, a sense of purpose evolves together with a securing experience and narrative of interdependence. When I sense that the tribe needs me as much as I need the tribe, my security and feelings of well-being are greatly enhanced.

So often children and adolescents who have struggled along the developmental path (such as those in an intensive treatment setting) have lives inundated with others (particularly professionals) looking to "help" them. In the context of a child who has needed to *block care* due to a history of caretakers who have been unable to understand and/or meet their needs, this is problematic at best. Interestingly though, when these same relationally vulnerable children experience themselves as having something to offer others, it can be remarkably healing. Conversely, when a relationally vulnerable child has their lack of empathic attunement to another pointed out, it almost always activates shame and thrusts the child into a maladaptive regression and potential acting-out.

This being the case, the process of helping a child or adolescent move in the direction of service to the need(s) of others (finding meaning) must be approached with great care. Supporting a child in finding a sense of meaning is generally best done with a light hand, involving more affirmation from caretakers' observation of caring acts, rather than directing the child to be so engaged. When as caretakers we are able to support a child or adolescent in developing a narrative of meaningfulness through noting and affirming observed kindness or support to others, we pave the way for development in this last stage.

This is not to say that we cannot provide gentle direction towards a child's support of another, but in doing so we must be very careful to not elicit in the child a sense of shame for what they have not done on their own. If we can suggest that the child has special capacities to be helpful, it can sometimes support self-esteem in a manner that allows the child to move towards an act of helpfulness (e.g. "Sonny would not let anyone else into the quiet room when he is this upset, but I suspect he trusts you enough to allow you in to help him calm down" or, "These boxes are so heavy that there are not many kids who could help with them, but with those guns [slang for muscles] of yours, I know you could").

As noted with all three stages, children and adolescents will progress and regress in their development dependent upon a wide range of variables. It is also important (again) to note that a child's development within this model may differ greatly from relationship to relationship. For example, a teenage girl may be involved in a deeply connected relationship with a boyfriend, engaged in all three stages of development, while with her parents she is still very much stuck at stage one.

Examples of interactions supporting a child's sense of purpose and meaning

» "Sue, could you help Mary with her math today? You are so good at this and I think she would let you help her in a way that she would not let me."

» "Buddy, I saw you get off the bus today and how you helped the little guy behind you down the big step—you are such a good and kind guy."

» Caretaker: "I know you were really mad at me when you were in the quiet room today, but when I came in, recognizing that I am pregnant and a little sensitive to being hurt, you sat down on the floor so as to not have me be frightened."

Child: "That's not why I did that, I don't care if you are frightened of me, as matter of fact I like it if you and your stupid baby are scared of me."

Caretaker: "OK, maybe that is true but what I felt was an angry kid who even though angry still had the ability to think about me and do something kind."

» "You three guys are the most powerful in the room and when I see you treat Bobby, who is not very powerful, with kindness I so respect you guys."

For an eloquent discussion on the role of *purpose and community* within child and adolescent milieus, the reader is encouraged to explore Lou Cozolino's two books, *The Social Neuroscience of Education* (2013) (most appropriate for clinicians) and *Attachment-Based Teaching: Creating a Tribal Classroom* (2014a) (appropriate for clinicians and front-line staff). Even though these text are ostensibly written for those working in education, their crystalline insights concerning the power of the means of creating community apply directly to clinical milieus.

Conclusion

The use of the construction metaphor presented earlier is in no way to suggest that **no** work can be done on the upper floors while the foundation is still shaky. Some work above may be helpful and can even support the foundational work. The children we serve in intensive treatment programs are always a moving target with respect to these developmental needs. This fact demands of caretakers the ability for empathic attunement to inform their approach to the child, trying intervention at one level and if not succeeding, generally shifting to a focus on a lower level. This level of sophisticated attunement and flexibility is demanding and requires a framework to both understand the level or nature of the child's needs and effective strategies to meet them.

The balance of this text will offer insights and strategies associated with meeting these developmental needs. Within the treatment milieu, the age level served will have some impact on how this work is done, but in many respects very little. The difference between working with children of distinct ages lies largely in how you meet the need, not in the need itself. Children at different ages will require the packaging of our care in a distinct manner or our efforts will not be accessible to them. Younger children generally require clearer, less abstract efforts at supporting development and older children somewhat more abstract. This is not always the case but for the most part is true, meaning that the nature of interactions with children and adolescents often needs to be distinct or you will run the risk of the teenager feeling infantilized in a manner that elicits shame and embarrassment.

The text that follows will offer many insights and strategies useful in this work and applicable within this developmental model.

SUPPORTING HEALING ATTACHMENTS IN THE TREATMENT MILIEU

How Is an Attachment-Informed Approach Used in a Child and Adolescent Treatment Milieu?

Chapter 5

HOW ARE ATTACHMENTS FORMED AND HOW IS THIS APPLIED IN THE TREATMENT MILIEU?

As suggested within our definition, *attachments* develop within the context of relational experience and become a part of our emotional and cognitive make-up on both a conscious and an unconscious level. The ability to enjoy strong or positive attachments throughout life is significantly linked to the nature of our connections during childhood, with the heaviest loading for impact during the first three years. This is not to suggest that early attachment difficulties are irreversible but rather, if unresolved, they point social and emotional development in a highly problematic direction. A child's early experiences shape both the development of their brains and the nature of their expectations and openness to attachment. Again, this is not to suggest that early life experiences leave an immutable stamp on a child's capacity to form and use relationships; but it is to say that what happens in those first years is profoundly important and may take many years of compassionate and attuned connections to correct and "rewire" if things have not gone well.

In that childhood is our principle focus and childhood experiences are critical to attachment style and/or capacity, we will direct most of our attention to early life attachment development. It is, however, important to acknowledge that most insights with respect to attachment apply equally to adults and children. For those interested in the adult-to-adult side of attachment, I recommend the works of Sue Johnson, Daniel Siegel and Lou Cozolino.

As we attempt to understand how attachments are formed in the child–adult dyad, our attention must first turn to understanding the profound degree of dependency on the part of the human infant upon their caretaker. From a developmental perspective our species' maturation towards self-sufficiency lags dramatically behind that of all others, resulting in a profound human need for a durable and mutually reinforcing relationship between the infant and their caretaker. In the absence of such a bond both the infant and in time our species would perish.

So what is it that the infant does for the parent, and the parent for the infant that promotes and preserves attachment and the adult's commitment to caregiving? From the moment a woman becomes aware of her pregnancy, the typical mother begins to form an empathic and protective relationship with her unborn child. The mother, if secure in her own attachments and not overwhelmed by other variables, begins to feel a profound commitment to protect the child from harm and promote its growth. In the fulfillment of this commitment, the mother is afforded a sense of purpose, pride and competency as she is guided by her empathic caring for the child and the child's growth.

At birth the dance of attachment between mother and infant typically, when not impeded by factors such as maternal mental illness and environmental stress, fully launches as the mother is overwhelmed with wonder at what she has created and the child shows a significant preference for the smell, sight and touch of mom. When this process goes well, the attuned care of the infant rewards mom with everything from pride in the child's thriving to the glow and warmth associated with the flow of oxytocin (a hormone promoting a powerful sense of well-being) within the mom as she cuddles and feeds her little one. For the child, food, safety, warmth and perhaps their own boost of oxytocin drives a longing for the attachment forward.

As time passes, if all goes well, the child begins to understand their ability to impact the parent and draw the parent into supportive behaviors. The parent smiles back when the child smiles, frowns when the child is sad, and feeds, changes, comforts or plays with the child when the child is crying or acting cranky. **This dance carries on in one form or another over the course of childhood, when things go well.**

In this developmental process the child develops a secure and safe sense when the parent is present. Over time, however, due to experiences of optimal frustration (see below), children begin to develop an increasing belief in their own competencies and the ability to soothe themselves through reliance upon the emotional memories of their caretaker and an evolving set of self-soothing strategies. In other words, the child develops from a sense of safety based upon the competent caretaker's physical presence and care, to safety associated with trust in their own evolving capacities and the ability to feel safe in accessing the emotional memory of the competent caretaker.

In short, attachments within a young child's life evolve as the child and caretaker experience (for the most part or "good enough") a mutually gratifying process of connection; both feeling a secure sense of well-being within the relationship. As we try to understand more specifically how it is that attachments deepen over time and use this understanding to direct our work with children, we will draw from many developmental theorists and researchers.

We will start this discussion with a brief overview of three core concepts concerning attachment development largely taken from the work of Dan Hughes (2007). The first of these is *intersubjectivity*, the second represented in the acronym *PACE* (playful, accepting, curious and empathic) and the third in the attachment-strengthening process of *Connect–Tear–Repair*.

> *Note:* Again, please be aware that throughout this text the term "caretaker" is used in a generic sense to describe anyone in the position to care for a child, including but not limited to: parents, foster-parents, older siblings, extended family, teachers, therapists and even law enforcement personnel.

Intersubjectivity

At the core of supporting the attachment process is a highly intimate shared experience referred to in the attachment literature as *intersubjectivity* (Stern 1985). In simple terms, this shared experience is a deep, albeit transient, sense of "feeling felt" or lost together for a moment in a common feeling and experience. This shared sense of the moment is largely non-verbal and reflects a non-hierarchical connection of oneness in focus, thought and feeling. These moments come and go, yet build upon one another over time to provide a transcendent sense of shared self, deep connection and caring.

Intersubjective moments can occur in the context of a wide variety of experiences. They can evolve early in a courtship relationship as a young couple stays up all night talking, losing sense of time and feeling more at home with one another than alone. They can occur in a moment of play between a father and a son as the milkweed stalks become light sabers and they vanquish the frog king living in the pond. They can occur in the sharing of deep sorrow over the loss of a loved one, as wordless embraces allow two mourners to collapse into a hug. They can occur in the joyful laughter of a little one playing peek-a-boo, or a particularly well acted-out story of "This little pig went to market." They can occur between a mother and a daughter in the gentle hug offered as they take a last look at a home they have loved and are leaving. They can occur between an infant and his mother as they settle into each other's arms for a last snuggle before being laid in bed for the night. And so on and so on...

At the core of the intersubjective moment is connection without hierarchy, without purpose (aside from that of connecting), experienced within and between both individuals equally. So often in the lives of our more complicated children, struggling on so many fronts, the number and quality of intersubjective moments is quite limited. In recognizing this fact and the importance of these experiences in wiring the brain for connection, emotional regulation and well-being, we are compelled as caretakers and caretaking institutions to seek, value and promote opportunities for intersubjectivity. Sadly, the pace and demands of our current world, as well as our reluctance to value that which cannot be easily measured, serve to undermine our culture's value and provision of this deeply human capacity and need for moments of all-encompassing connection.

Intersubjective connection, whether between a parent and a child or a clinician and a child, requires a deep commitment to supporting the child in "feeling felt," whether this be in joyfulness or sadness. Dan Hughes, who writes as eloquently as anyone on this topic, describes intersubjectivity as demanding three shared components: shared attention, shared affect and shared intention. In the sharing of these domains there evolves a transient "oneness" that virtually defines intimacy and connection.

It is additionally important to recognize that a child's evolving sense of self is largely created by the caretaker–child experiences of intersubjectivity. When the caretaker experiences the child with delight, they experience themselves as delightful; but conversely, the opposite experience can also be true: If your parents are bored with you, you are boring; if they are often angry with you, you are bad. For the most part the children served in intensive treatment settings have *selves* they largely perceive as negative, given that they have evolved from negative caretaker–child experiences. In turn, these negative selves entrench and block the child from the very openness to care and intersubjectivity that could allow for healing of their disturbed self and the rewriting of their relational stories.

PACE

The **PACE** model offered by Dan Hughes (2007) for facilitating attachment between caretaker and child prescribes an adult stance of **P**layfulness, **A**cceptance, **C**uriosity and **E**mpathy. Hughes suggests that it is through this stance that critical moments of intersubjectivity and deepening attachment evolve. These moments are void of power differentials or any clear agenda on the adult's part to teach, or direct, in deference to the far more important effort to simply be present and connect. It is the caretaker's ability to walk beside the child, to be with them in their inner world in a safe and accepting manner, that allows the adult the capacity to support the child through periods of powerful emotional upheaval or stress. The caretaker's attunement and acceptance of the child's inner world allows them to support emotional co-regulation (see Chapter 2) and ultimately promote the critical capacity to self-regulate in a manner that facilitates learning and higher-level adaptive functioning.

Within the PACE directive there is no implied hierarchy or sequence for these modes of interaction. The PACE stance simultaneously reflects all four modes of interaction with some degree of primary focus vacillating among them dependent upon an attuned sense of what is needed to further the connection within the moment. In other words, the situation in which one finds oneself and the child's response to our efforts to connect will dictate whether playfulness, acceptance, curiosity or empathy is utilized. The fact is that one may move between these avenues for connection in a fluid, non-sequential manner; in essence, PACE describes a *stance* towards the child, requiring the adult to seek the avenue that best fits the child and the moment. This PACE stance is critical to all aspects of caretaking; in short, it is useful to think of PACE as an interactional posture for which we strive within all situations, particularly when needing to set a behavioral limit or dealing with a dysregulated child.

Offered below is an overview of the PACE model to introduce the concept and to apply it within clinical settings. The reader is encouraged to see Hughes (2009) for a more in-depth discussion of PACE.

Playfulness within the treatment milieu

Playfulness, or the "P" of the PACE acronym, is an often overlooked, yet extremely powerful aspect of the attachment-enhancing process. In being playful, caretaker and child enter into a highly intimate, intersubjective or jointly created experience of the moment. As we pretend together that the game of peek-a-boo surprises us each time that the other reappears; that the family dog is speaking with us, sharing human-like thoughts and feelings; as we share our concern for a stuffed bunny's ear and the possible need for him to go to the bunny doctor, we enter into an intersubjective (largely right-brained) form of connection. In these moments, we are saying, "Here are my playful thoughts and fantasies, can you join me? Can we go together to a place as equals, devoid of power differentials, governed by nothing more than a desire to engage one another, pretend and/or laugh?" The intersubjective nature of play is a powerful platform from which to build attachment.

Playfulness is most often accessible in situations where individuals feel safe; yet reciprocally, playfulness can at times be effective in eliciting a sense of safety. Playfulness is an act of vulnerability, stepping away from an offensive or defensive stance towards connection for the sake of connection. It can play out in everything from passing moments between strangers (e.g. as I ask one of the many dogs led by their owners passing my home, "How are you today, buddy?"), to an intimate moment between mother and child as they play peek-a-boo or engage in play with a stuffed animal.

A child and their caretaker's engagement with a favorite stuffed animal is a common form of important play that often occurs over and over in supporting attachment. The child and caretaker's relationship with "Bunny" serves as an important bridge to intimacy through their shared (playful) delusion that he is very, very real. In other words, in joining the child in pushing aside any sense that Bunny is but cloth, stuffing and thread and embracing his need to go to the doctor or to have tea, or his love of gymnastics, the adult and child say to one another, "Forget the rest of the world, you and I have created our own." There are few dynamics more intimate or bonding than the fanciful *co-creation of a world*.

The importance of playfulness in strengthening attachments noted, it is critical to recognize that this is true **only** when the sense of fun and joy in the play is reciprocal. Although silliness and teasing can fall into the category of play, when there is a power differential expressed or sought through the interaction it is **not likely** to lead to intersubjectivity and strengthened attachments. Teasing that belittles (e.g. "I've seen turtles run faster than you") or is used in an effort to direct another (e.g. "If you keep eating so much candy you are going to get too big to pass through the door") is not typically supportive to connection. In fact, under the guise of "playfulness," hurtful teasing and sarcasm can too often enter the caretaker–child dynamic in a way that is profoundly damaging to the child's sense of safety in the relational connection.

Playfulness can take many forms, but at its core is the expression of light-heartedness, a limited sense of urgency, a lack of power differential and a joyful sense of pleasure in connecting. Different individuals will approach playfulness in distinct ways. There is no one avenue through which to be playful. If the effort at a playful interaction seems to lighten the child's spirit or draws a playful response, it is probably helpful; if the child seems agitated or withdrawn in response, it is not likely to be supportive to attachment and/or co-regulation.

It is important to realize that even though playfulness can be a wonderful and compassionate manner of connecting, it can also be experienced as a form of missed empathy, even when done well. When a child is feeling unsafe and/or lost in their emotions, an effort at playfulness may be off-putting. In these situations, a persistent effort to engage in a playful manner may serve to increase a child's sense of being misunderstood and alone, and so it is imperative that we shift our interaction away from playfulness, towards acceptance, curiosity or empathy, recognizing that playfulness is not an option at this moment.

Again, this is not to suggest that playfulness cannot be used to connect supportively with agitated children and adolescents, for there are youngsters and situations in which playfulness can be quite connecting and extremely supportive to their emotional regulation. It is possible when dealing with a highly agitated child to attempt being playful in making silly or ridiculous or somewhat self-deprecating comments. Again, as noted above, one must carefully read the child's cues in this effort to determine if they are calming or agitating. If agitating, it is imperative to apologize and move to a different strategy.

Offered below is an example of a conversation that might play out with an agitated child in attempting to connect and support them in calming. This approach is done embracing the fact that the **only** task at hand when dealing with a highly agitated child is to support their emotional regulation; **this is not a teachable moment** or a time to focus on accountability. Once the child is regulated, issues such as accountability can (carefully) be revisited with them when their brains are ready for learning.

The setting is a hospital quiet room where a 15-year-old male is enraged and screaming, "I am going to f...ing kill all of you and your families!" The staff member enters the room attempting to avoid any appearance of intimidation or power differential. He is hoping to distract the child from interpersonal tension and direct the focus towards a somewhat absurd observation, allowing the child's affect to back down a notch.

Caretaker: "Man, something has really made you angry."

Child: "No shit, asshole! Get out of here before I f...ing knock you out."

Caretaker: "I get it, you just want me out of here! But I can't go because we have a rule that says we don't leave really upset kids alone without some support, so I am just going to sit down and shut up and try not to bug you."

After a few minutes of quiet, perhaps attempting to engage the child in tossing a ball or some other non-verbal activity, the clinical caretaker might look at his shoes and say something like:

Caretaker: "Boy, I just couldn't figure out what color of socks to wear this morning. I put on black ones and didn't like how they looked, then blue ones, then no socks and here I am with these black ones and really don't like how they look."

Child: "You're a f...ing idiot! I don't care about your f...ing socks!"

Caretaker: "Yeah you may be right, I am a little over the top with this sock thing. Still, I worry people might judge me for my poor choice of colors."

Child: "You really are an idiot, I am in here threatening to kill people and you're talking about your f...ing socks. Man, you are more f...ed up than me!"

Caretaker: "You may be right. Please don't mention this sock thing to the rest of the staff, I don't want them to figure out what you seem to already know..."

At this point the clinical caretaker might make an effort to engage the child in a more direct manner:

Caretaker: "Can you tell me what happened, why you are so angry? I know something must have really bothered you. You don't act like this for no reason..."

This kind of absurdity or playfulness can be a powerful step away from the tension of the moment, supporting a dysregulated child lost in anger and longing for retaliation. In attempting this kind of playful intervention to support the dysregulated child, it is imperative that the adult be well regulated and have only the agenda to connect with the child and support them in calming. If in attempting to use playfulness it appears to further agitate the child, it is important to quickly move away from this strategy towards acceptance, curiosity or empathy.

Each individual will approach *playfulness* in a different manner, some more overt and silly, others more subtle. In the expression of playfulness one's non-verbals carry much of the invitation to play along and must be consistent with one's words. A smile or an exaggerated or inappropriate non-verbal expression often serves as the initial invitation to playfulness. Whatever the caretaker's playful effort, it will be useful in supporting a sense of connection as long as the child experiences it as a non-threatening invitation to a shared moment with no purpose aside from playfulness. This may occur within a range of dynamics and/or emotional states from neutral to emotionally loaded, and may vary from simple silliness and pretending to more sophisticated observation of irony.

The majority of children coming into intensive treatment do so from settings in which caretakers (parents, teachers, clinicians) have been confused and overwhelmed by the child's behavior and needs, often communicating apprehension, bewilderment and fear (e.g. "We are all just so worried about your poor decisions!"). Although understandable, the impact of these verbal and non-verbal expressions of concern often serve to heighten the child's anxiety and shame and reinforce negative self-narratives.

As a result, the majority of children within these settings have a response to caretaker apprehension or worried concern that is largely negative, eliciting irritation, emotional withdrawal and aggressive acting-out. For these children, who are operating with limited self-esteem, debilitating shame and struggles with hopelessness, the caretaker's worried concern is experienced as intolerably critical, serving to push them away from the very emotional connection and support needed for their healing.

A gentle *playful* approach with a struggling child, even if not initially accepted, rarely elicits a negative reaction (e.g. "You clearly have not been making your best decisions, but it could be worse, you haven't taken up wrestling gators!"). When an institutional or non-institutional caretaker is able to convey the level of acceptance, comfort and safety associated with gentle playfulness, the child is far more prone to experience them as powerful and caring. Typically, when a child experiences their caretaker as playful, they sense themselves as respected and enjoyed, allowing an implicit sense of relational hope so often lacking for that child.

This is not to suggest that playfulness can always be applied to further relational connection or in support of a child's de-escalation for there are times when, if not used carefully, playfulness can be experienced as a problematic empathic miss. The key to the effective use of playfulness or humor is in reading the child's reaction and using this to either continue on the path or back away from the tack. This attunement together with the child's clear experience of the caretaker's use of playfulness as having no purpose aside from that of connecting in an intersubjective moment often opens doors of connection.

(This does not mean that a skillful caretaker could not use playfulness to connect in a manner that ultimately serves in gaining some degree of behavioral compliance.)

When a treatment setting can honor and support playfulness and recognize its importance in promoting connection and conveying hope, it has great potential to reduce the number of power struggles and create a far more positive milieu. When playfulness is a valued form of interaction within the milieu, played out among staff and administration, clinicians and patients, parents and children, the overall effectiveness of the treatment program will almost always improve.

Examples of the expression of playfulness

» Imaginative play, e.g. "Oh, poor Bunny, he hurt his ear!", "I'm Superman and you are...," "We are in the last five seconds of the NBA playoffs and..."

» Silliness, e.g. puns, funny faces, exaggerated responses.

» Self-deprecation, e.g. "Oh my goodness, I am such a space shot—I wonder if I am actually from Mars," "Please don't listen to me today, I am so tired I could say anything."

» Physical humor, e.g. monkey gestures, exaggerated falling down.

» Unexpected behavior, e.g. "Is that a giraffe looking in the window?," "Oh, this book is so boring I think I will try reading it upside down."

» The use of silly nicknames, e.g. "Anna Banana," "Alligator Head."

Playfulness can be a wonderful way into connection. Whether dealing with a well-regulated or agitated child, this avenue can provide a gentle pathway into connecting and healing intersubjectivity.

Acceptance within the treatment milieu

Acceptance, or the "A" of the PACE acronym, refers to the importance of the caretaker's **unconditional acceptance** of a child's inner world (thoughts, perceptions and feelings). This does not entail the unconditional acceptance of behavior, but it does imply the acceptance of the thoughts and feelings that drive behavior. The acceptance by the clinical caretaker of an "unacceptable" or inaccurate thought or feeling is often counterintuitive and requires considerable restraint in avoiding the assumption of a corrective stance. A child's expression of negative or irrational beliefs and feelings (e.g. "I hate black people!", "All dogs bite!", "If you go I will die!", "You hate me!", "You wanted me to fail!") often elicit a strong moral and/or cognitively dissident reaction within caretakers, a reaction driven by the desire to help the child correct inaccurate or morally unacceptable aspects of their inner world.

It is understandable that caretakers who believe that a child's thoughts and feelings are driving problem behavior would wish to banish or "teach away" these aspects of the child's inner world. Unfortunately, however, it is often a caretaker's effort to change or correct the child's thoughts and feelings that elicits a sense of isolation and shame, promoting relational retreat and acting-out. When able to accept a child's inner world, the caretaker is in a position to support them in sorting through difficult thoughts and feelings without eliciting stifling shame and a defensive relational withdrawal.

One factor impacting a clinical caretaker's ability to accept a child's problematic thoughts and feelings is the caretaker's understanding and acceptance of their own inner world. This is an enormous topic, but suffice to say for our purpose that caretakers who are highly unaware or self-critical of their own inner worlds are not likely to be good at accepting the difficult inner world of a child. This issue will be discussed later in the section on identifying what gets in the way of attachment-informed work and what personal attributes are best suited for clinical work of this nature.

As noble as the clinical caretaker's motives may be in challenging a child's inaccurate and/or problematic thoughts and feelings, restraint in this corrective response in deference to *acceptance* is far more likely to be helpful. This restraint allows the child full expression of their inner world, as they clarify and experiment with thoughts and feelings in the safety of the caretaker's emotional presence. This acceptance allows the child to share their inner world without debilitating shame for "bad" thoughts and feelings as well as allowing the caretaker to better understand the child and ultimately help them decide for themselves what they think and feel.

When the clinical caretaker is able to marshal restraint and support the child in *feeling felt* prior to efforts at correction, the platform from which the caretaker operates is both better informed and more readily accepted. Greatly facilitating a caretaker's capacity to take this accepting stance is a committed belief that the child's inner world **always** makes sense in the context of their subjective experience.

Children need behavioral limits and logical consequences for their actions, but this does not apply to their thoughts and feelings. This does not mean that inappropriate **behavior** in the **expression** of the child's thoughts and feelings is acceptable, a distinction that is not always easy to manage. For example, it would be acceptable for a child to state with accompanying affect, "John hates me and I hate him too!" but probably not OK for them to say, "John hates me and I am going to f...ing kill him!" This is **not** to suggest that in response to this unacceptable threat the wise clinical caretaker will take on the dysregulated child's behavior in the moment. As will be discussed in the section on co-regulation and attachment-informed limit setting, the clinical caretaker's only responsibility with the dysregulated child is to help them calm; this is not a *teachable moment*; but once calm, the child may be able to learn from a gently presented consequence.

When a clinical caretaker is able to separate feelings from actions and *be* fully accepting of a child's dark, inaccurate and negative thoughts and emotions (e.g. rage, homicidal and suicidal ideation) while at the same time effectively setting limits on behavior, we walk the balance that truly promotes relational and emotional growth. Children need behavioral limits and logical consequences for their actions, as this helps them make sense of their world; **this does not apply to their thoughts and feelings**.

As noted earlier, for many caretakers, thoughts and feelings are understood as what drives problem behavior, therefore must be banished or "taught away." Unfortunately, it is a caretaker's inability to accept a child's difficult inner world of thoughts and feelings that leaves the child alone with them and more likely to act them out. When a child's caretaker is able to accept the child's inner world, it allows the child an opportunity to sort through thoughts and feelings with the caretaker's emotional support and facilitates a higher level of adaptive capacity.

As counterintuitive as it may be for clinical caretakers to say things such as, "Of course you wanted to hit Tom when he broke your new toy" or, " I know and I am sorry that you think that I don't care about you when I don't let you go to the gym when you are on level 1," the process of supporting a child in understanding that their thoughts and feelings are acceptable, even if acting on them is not, is a powerful expression of a caretaker's commitment to remain with them even when their internal world is not in a good place. As was discussed in the section in Chapter 3 concerning the function of attachment, it is only through a child's sense of a caretaker's ability to *feel their feelings* with them, the good and the bad, that the child develops the capacity to regulate their emotion. In other words, it is through the initial process wherein the caretaker and child co-regulate emotion that the child ultimately learns to self-regulate emotion. This *co-regulation* (which is discussed in more detail in Chapter 6) cannot occur if the caretaker cannot tolerate or accept the child's thoughts and feelings. The act of accepting distorted perceptions—the often quite critical and unpleasant thoughts and feelings of a child (frequently towards a competent and caring staff member)—is a tough but critical task in supporting a child's social, emotional and attachment growth. A clinical caretaker's ability to "be with" the child's sometimes disorganized and/or irrational inner world, as opposed to correcting them, is as critical to the attachment process as it is difficult.

In addition to the simple soothing power of *feeling felt*, the next step is in the caretaker supporting the child in *naming or labelling* their experience. This process supports right–left brain hemispheric integration and a more organized sense of their inner world. This noted, it is imperative that a **non-verbal** expression of accepting attunement precedes any effort to use language to communicate or name experiences.

Again, this stance is in no way supportive of permissive, indulgent caretaking in that children thrive within the structure of appropriate expectations and limits. This is a stance that helps children more openly express their inner worlds so that their caretakers can support them in learning to manage complicated and powerful thoughts and feelings. Within this model, children continue to be held appropriately accountable for their behavior but in the context of deeper understanding of what drives the behavior, and of acceptance on the part of the caretaker of their responsibility to support the child in learning to manage difficult thoughts and feelings.

The simple act of being emotionally present with a child or adolescent with an accepting stance as they share difficult thoughts and feelings is often our most powerful intervention. This noted, doing so can often be counterintuitive and very difficult when the temptation is to ask ourselves questions such as, "How is he going to learn if we don't correct his inaccurate or problematic thoughts and feelings?"; or make observations such as, "I can't just stand by and listen to what he says without responding; if I do, it is as if I agree with him." But we must remember that the vast majority of children and adolescents within an intensive treatment program have been bombarded with efforts to correct their thoughts and feelings to little benefit. In the final analysis, much of what we are hoping for children to develop are thoughts and feelings informed by empathy, but as wisely noted by Mary Gordon (2005, p.40), "empathy is caught, not taught." Acceptance of a child's or adolescent's inner world is often challenging, but when implemented is almost always powerful and healing.

Again, a factor critical to the emotional experience of acceptance by a child or adult relates to the nature of the other's non-verbal communication. The right brain being the origin of emotion, and non-verbals its language, words without accompanying and congruent emotion do not effectively register. As is discussed by Siegel and Bryson (2012) in *The Whole Brain Child*, a child's (or anyone's, for that matter) right brain content can only be felt, held and accepted by the caretaker's right brain.

This being the case, the expressed *acceptance* of emotionally laden thoughts and feelings must include non-verbal expression that reflects a similar affect. One cannot remain affectively non-reactive to the expression of another's powerful thoughts and feelings and have the other sense that they are accepted. As a child tearfully states, "I hate myself!" following some form of failure, a simple, kind, sad smile is likely to be more effective in expressing acceptance than a relatively emotionless statement, "I understand that right now you hate yourself." This is not to suggest that words cannot be used in the expression of acceptance, rather that words used without accompanying parallel non-verbal expression (the language of the right brain) are not effective in promoting connecting and healing intersubjectivity. In other words the caretakers effective expression must be consistent with their words. Perhaps the most effective response to a child's statement, "I hate myself!" is a gentle reflection, "Oh, buddy, it is so hard to have things not go well and to feel awful about yourself."

Our right brain to the child's right brain is the pathway to emotional communication capable of leading us to the expression of both acceptance, and judgment and non-acceptance. This being the case, and knowing the critical importance of the child's sense of *acceptance* when working with highly vulnerable and reactive children and adolescents, we **must** carefully monitor our non-verbal expressions.

Again, this is not to suggest that the right (emotional side) and left (language and rational side) of the brain are not both important in the context of relationship and facilitating higher-level adaptive functioning. It is the right brain to right brain connection that constitutes interpersonal traction, it is the left brain's naming and telling of the story that brings coherency to the child's inner world; yet let it be clear that in the absence of traction, no amount of left-brain power is going to drive adaptive functioning forward.

Examples of the expression of acceptance

» "Of course you feel..."

» Non-verbal expression of acceptance and emotional availability, e.g. soft smile, gentle concern.

» "I know there is a reason for what you did, we don't do things for no reason."

» "I know it is so hard."

» "Oh, how you hate it when..."

» "This is so difficult for you!"

» "You are really angry and sad right now and the only thing you can think about is how nice it would be to just not be here anymore." (Response to suicidal comments.)

» "What Mr. S. did felt awful to you and made you really want to hurt him back!"

Curiosity within the treatment milieu

Curiosity, or the "C" of the PACE acronym, entails the caretaker's expression of deep interest in the child's inner and outer life. In approaching a child with curiosity, it is critically important to recognize that this has the power to promote attachment **only** if done in tandem with acceptance. Should a caretaker express curiosity concerning a child's inner world in the absence of unconditional acceptance of their thoughts and feelings, it will be experienced as the subtle, or not so subtle, gathering of evidence as part of an emotional indictment; a process that is destructive to the child–caretaker connection. A child's sense that there are acceptable and unacceptable thoughts and feelings sets the stage for the sharing of only those aspects of their inner world they believe to be acceptable and/or the misrepresentation of their thoughts and feelings to fit those endorsed by the caretaker.

Both attachment and insight are enhanced when a caretaker is able to express curiosity in an effort to understand the child through comments such as, "Can you try to tell me what you were thinking when you swore at your teacher?" or, "Buddy, what's up, you seem really upset?", or, "I bet you have a lot of feelings about what just happened, probably some pretty mad and sad ones, am I right?" or, "I understand that you're really angry at me and probably want me to just leave you alone, did I get that right?" In the process of expressing our curiosity, it is imperative that we honor the child's inability or unwillingness to share their thoughts and feelings, for if unable to accept their limitations or reluctance to share their thoughts and feelings, we are out of the gate disengaging from an accepting stance.

The sharing of thoughts and feelings with another for both adults and children, when not clear how they will be perceived, or how comfortable we are with them ourselves, requires a high degree of safety and anticipation of acceptance from those with whom we might share. Too often a child's lack of a sense of emotional safety and/or acceptance translates into a fear of consequences for their negative thoughts and feelings and an unwillingness to share them. Alternatively, the child opts to misrepresent them in a manner in line with what they believe others wish to hear; a choice which effectively leaves them alone with a sense of shame for their thoughts and feelings. Again, *acceptance* of the child's inner world determines whether the caretaker's *curiosity* will be allowed by the child to open the door to more deeply and lovingly knowing the child.

Much more could be said concerning the misapplication of "curiosity" and a child's reluctance to reveal anything in the context of a superficial exchange or a seemingly unsafe situation. (e.g. Parent: "What did you do at school today?" Child: "Nothing.") Surprisingly, however, with acceptance and patience (not rushing them to do so), children can be quite self-disclosing when interacting with an accepting/safe adult even if disclosure may result in consequences for behavior but not negative judgment of underlying self.

Few factors serve more effectively to promote a safe and deep sense of connection than the experience of another as both deeply interested (curious) and accepting, whether within a treatment program, family, school or therapy session. It is often this experience more than any other that allows for social and emotional growth and healing.

Most of us have a sense of the relational draw of an accepting and curious other, and how curiosity from another is affirming. Who has not had the experience of feeling somewhat unimportant and disengaged when visiting with someone who seems uninterested in our lives? (E.g. the scene in the film *Beaches* in which Bette Midler's character, a self-absorbed woman, chatters on about herself until she realizes that she is doing all of the talking and responds by saying, "Enough about me! Now, what do *you* think about me?")

All of us, from time to time, find ourselves in complicated situations forced to choose between the lesser of two bad options. How different is our experience of the observation of others in these situations when we sense acceptance and curiosity concerning our choice, vs. judgment! The children and adolescents we serve in the intensive treatment setting are constantly facing difficult situations, pulled between inner dynamics (e.g. a deeply held belief that I should trust no one vs. a profound longing for loving care) and social dilemmas (e.g. aligning with my peers and protecting important friendships vs. doing what the staff want me to and maybe going home sooner). When as a clinical caretaker we seek to understand a child's or adolescent's difficult dilemma in such situations with acceptance and curiosity, the caretaker learns far more and the child is not left alone with these difficult situations, thoughts and feelings.

Curiosity tells a child that they matter and that you are interested in them, that you believe that what they think, feel and do makes sense and is understandable. In this relational stance the child is supported in trying to make sense of their own often complicated and confusing inner worlds and is not alone in the process. The process of walking beside a child as they sort through their difficult thoughts and feelings affords them the critical opportunity to figure out who they are while feeling supported and cared for, as opposed to judged and frightened.

Too often, both directly and indirectly we convey to children that their inner lives do not make sense and in doing so leave them with a sense of abandonment, hopelessness and shame, often setting the stage for them to think of themselves as bad and/or simply as a random set of incoherent thoughts, feelings and behaviors. It is the expression of our ability to reflect back to a child that they *make sense*, even if neither we nor they may understand it in the moment, that sets the stage for their important process of developing a coherent self-narrative (discussed further in Chapter 9) and an evolving core-organized sense of self. The expression of accepting-curiosity, perhaps better than any other form of interaction, conveys the critical message "I believe you make sense and I want to know you better," thus affirming worth and integrity to the child's sense of self.

Examples of the expression of curiosity

> »   "Can you help me understand what you are feeling or thinking?"

> »   "I want to understand this better. Can you help me?"

> »   "You do things for a reason. Can you help me understand why you...?"

> »   "I know you may not be sure why you..., but I bet you have some ideas about why you...?"

> »   "You really deserve to have people understand why you... Can you help me understand?"

> »   "It looks so hard feeling that. I really want to understand why."

Empathy within the treatment milieu

Empathy, or the "E" of the PACE acronym, must be as present as possible in all that we do, expressed in non-verbal communication, language and actions. Empathy entails a process through which we sense, and to some extent experience and accept, another's inner life. Empathy is **not** an endorsement of the other's thoughts or feelings, but rather a deep emotionally connected sense that we understand and accept the thoughts and feelings of another.

It is empathy that affords us our greatest sense of what it is to be another and provides emotional insight into what it is that they might want or need from us. The sense that one is not alone, that there is another present and capable of making us "feel felt," is the initial key step to our learning to manage emotion and regulate affect.

Almost equal to the developmental value of being the recipient of empathy is a child's evolving capacity to direct empathy towards others. This ability allows for the relational world to be less confusing, as empathic awareness of others provides important understanding of their thoughts, feelings and motivations.

Again, in the words of Mary Gordon (2005, p.40), "empathy is caught, not taught," therefore the process of supporting children in the development of critical capacity for empathy towards others is contingent upon the caretaker's capacity to infuse empathic attunement into as many caretaker–child interactions as possible. Children who have been well cared for, having had their needs empathically understood and met by an attuned caretaker, generally find empathic connection comforting. Empathic connection with children with less attuned backgrounds, however, is often far more difficult in that they may well push back from allowing themselves to "feel felt" by others, until they have had enough positive experiences to allow for a level of trust, intimacy and appreciation for the efforts of an attuned other.

Empathy with and for the troubled child

Our capacity as caretakers to offer essential empathic attunement can be very difficult when dealing with a complex, challenging and/or defiant child such as served within an intensive treatment setting. The question becomes, "How do I empathize with a child who is being hostile towards me and/or does not want me to be emotionally close?" Again, the answer generally lies in the redoubled effort on the part of the caretaker to remember that the child's behavior makes sense in the context of their past experience and developmental stage. If they want to push us away when we wish nothing but to be helpful, our empathic awareness must honor the coherency of their response, yet remain as available as they are able to tolerate without becoming negatively reactive.

This process of honoring, but not fully being controlled by a child's desire to push away empathic efforts, entails our learning how to be present and open to the child without pushing in a manner that significantly activates their defensive responses. This is a delicate balance and often involves beginning the process with no words and no directives, simply expressing a willingness to be with the child and quietly attempt to feel the feelings that are impacting them. When the child is in an agitated, anxious, confused or frightened state, their behavior is ruled by a focus upon nothing other than safety and the likely deployment of the fight, flight or freeze response. In these moments, there is little opportunity for engagement of the upper or right brain through language and reason; there is no learning that will take place. The **only** task at hand is that of helping the child to feel safe and become regulated and thus able to move back into their upper brain and the ability to think and learn.

The role of empathy in supporting a child's developing capacity for emotional regulation cannot be overstated and begins with what Daniel Stern (1985) refers to as the caretaker matching the vitality of the dysregulated child's affect, in other words accurately reflecting the child's affect while at the same time remaining emotionally regulated. (The reflection in the mirror is vibrating, but the mirror remains still.) In this accurate, yet regulated and accepting reflection of the child's tumultuous inner world, the terrifying sense of being overwhelmed begins to abate, to be replaced by a sense of being relationally held, safe and in time able to re-engage the more adaptive and sophisticated upper brain's ability to problem solve (see Chapter 9 for more on this topic). This is in many respects analogous to a small rushing tributary passing down the steep side of a canyon bound for envelopment in the river below, the urgency and frenetic force of the small racing stream (child's dysregulated affect) feeding into the river (caretaker's regulated but open stance) with ease and acceptance, moving still in the same direction, yet quietly held by the river.

Although empathy in and of itself can be enormously supportive in helping a child learn to manage emotion and strengthen attachments, its application in informing our behavioral expectations for a child is also extremely important. It is often our empathic awareness of a child's inner world that allows us to understand and respond to their needs, abilities and limitations. It is our empathically accessed knowledge of what the child can and cannot tolerate that best informs our effort to provide growth-enhancing experiences. As will be discussed in the section below on Heinz Kohut's (1971) concept of *optimal frustration*, it is the caretaker's empathic attunement to the child that allows them to challenge the child in a manner that affords the child an evolving sense of competency and self-assurance, as opposed to the enfeeblement associated with consistently over- or under-challenging a child.

Empathy as a shared felt experience is an avenue for knowing a child deeply and cannot be overstated as a critical aspect in the caretaker–child connection within the treatment setting. In the absence of good empathic attunement, even the most caring of caretakers will miss the mark concerning the child's wants, needs and abilities, and the relationship or functional attachment between the child and caretaker will suffer.

Impediments to empathic connection

Three broad factors are generally involved in failed caretaker–child empathic connection: 1. child–caretaker temperamental mismatch; 2. highly distinct child–caretaker experiential background; and 3. caretaker emotional vulnerability and dysregulation. Each of these will be discussed below.

Child–caretaker temperamental mismatch is a common obstacle to empathic attunement on the part of an otherwise competent and compassionate caretaker. Temperament refers to one's inborn neurobiological wiring expressed in predominate emotional, cognitive and interpersonal styles. Examples of these kind of traits include *emotionality* (how open one is in the expression of emotion), *interpersonal physicality* (how open one is to touch) and *introversion vs. extroversion*, to mention a few. The more similar a child and their caretaker with respect to temperament, the more likely the caretaker is to accurately read the child's cues. When this goes well, accurate attunement plays out, the child *feels felt* and the caretaker is able to make sense of the child's behavior.

When temperamental mismatch sets the stage for the caretaker to misperceive the child's inner world and needs, however, the empathic miss can lead to a range of unfortunate unintended outcomes. For example, if a caretaker finds physical support such as a hug a source of comfort when upset, reads an upset child as needing a hug but the child is temperamentally limited in their ability to accept or tolerate touch, the situation will deteriorate rapidly with both the child and caretaker feeling confused and misunderstood. Unfortunately, this kind of dynamic plays out often and is at the root of many caretaker-child struggles in the treatment setting and family.

Another factor often undermining empathic attunement relates to differences between *child and caretaker in their experiential backgrounds and cultures*. It is largely from our experience and culture that interpretation of another's behavior is derived. Should I have grown up in a family where physical safety was never at doubt, I am likely to experience a caretaker's playful poke as an expression of affection. Should I have grown up in a household where physical aggression was prominent, however, this same poke may be experienced as a prelude to abuse. Again, should this playful poke result in an agitated/angry child, the empathic bridge is endangered as both the child and the caretaker sense confusion and feelings of being misunderstood.

A third factor often undermining capacity for empathic attunement is the *caretaker's emotional state* at a given time. Empathy entails a shift in attention away from one's own thoughts, feelings and needs towards the inner experience of another. Making this shift depends significantly on our own internal state with regard to feelings of safety and emotional security. If we are not adequately secure in these regards, it is difficult to shift the focus from our state of being to that of another. In some respects we must be able to put our own adaptive needs on autopilot while we attend to those of another; if we should be in the middle of an emotional storm, turning on the autopilot to attend to another is both counterintuitive and in some situations ill advised and even dangerous, if not impossible.

A common factor undermining a caretaker's emotional availability for empathy is linked to the caretaker's own vulnerable self-esteem. If the caretaker should have a significant need for the child to affirm, or at least not challenge, some vulnerable aspect of their sense of self, a challenge to this realm of the caretaker will often short-circuit empathy.

A classic example of this involves a caretaker who struggles with self-esteem concerning their own core competency, encountering a child who disregards their authority, thus activating a retaliatory or defensive vs. empathic response on the caretaker's part.

Clearly, all of us are from time to time going to get blindsided by our own underlying vulnerability and respond to a challenging child in a manner lacking the empathy that is so critical to our being wise, compassionate and effective. This is life and what it is to be human, and not a reason for despair; however, it is an important time for self-reflection and the seeking of a trusted other to better understand and manage our vulnerabilities. This need, when working with highly challenging others such as the children and adolescents within an intensive treatment setting, demands the ready availability of supportive clinical supervisors to help us work through such issues. It is inevitable (as humans) that we will encounter others with whom we struggle emotionally; this is not an issue within a treatment setting as long as we are aware of these issues and work them through with supportive others. The relational recovery and repair from these moments of lost empathy is both necessary and possible and will be discussed in the section below on relational repair.

Empathy is an aspect of the PACE model that must at all times be playing in the background informing our approach to a child. Our empathic attunement will determine our application of the PACE stance, guiding our understanding of the child and which aspect of PACE is most helpful in a given moment. Can I lead with playfulness, or should I go with the simple open expression of acceptance, or empathic affective reflection? It is our empathic attunement and response to a child's or adolescent's thoughts, feelings and needs that makes the treatment setting a place of healing.

Examples of the expression of empathy

- » Gentle touch.
- » Matched affect (largely non-verbal).
- » Touching one's heart while listening or speaking.
- » "Oh how hard this is!"

» "I am sorry this is so difficult!"

» "I so wish this was different, I really want you to feel better!"

Conclusion on PACE

A PACE stance in relationship to a child is not always easy, nor does it always result in behavioral compliance or emotional regulation. Oftentimes challenges in the treatment setting and in ourselves may make this stance difficult to carry forward; nonetheless, when embraced as a core stance for how we want to interact with children, it opens doors to connection or attachment that are healing and otherwise inaccessible.

If it is relational connection that we believe to be at the core of adaptive growth and well-being, then it is a PACE stance that represents both the road to health and the pathway back to this road when life has led a child into the ditch. PACE is not about permissiveness or giving the child what they want. PACE is a stance with which to understand a child's needs and to meet them in a manner expressing respect, minimizing debilitating shame, and affording a sense of being understood and appreciated. In this model, support to a child in connecting, growing and healing is tied to the caretaker's expression of unconditional caring (love), and belief that the child's behavior *makes sense* and that they are doing the best they know how in the context of their experience, perceptions and feelings.

PACE is an effective means by which to keep a child feeling safely connected and in this state able to create a functional self-narrative, a concept discussed in more detail in Chapter 9. A caretaker's limitation in maintaining a PACE-informed relational stance is associated with many variables and is discussed in more detail later in the text; however, as a point of departure with regard to this critical capacity, three guidelines are offered:

1. Caretakers must practice self-reflection in their use of PACE and not allow themselves to simply blame the child for their own limitations.

2. Caretakers should always consider seeking support from trusted others when recognizing a limited ability to be PACE-like with a child.

3. Caretakers must have the capacity to forgive themselves when they miss the mark and repair the relationship through a genuine and emotionally attuned apology to the child.

Optimal frustration — supporting secure attachment, sense of self and evolving competency

The developmental concept of *optimal frustration* was first presented by Heinz Kohut (1971) in his discussion of the conditions necessary for a child to establish a stable, secure experience of self. Optimal frustration demands of the child's caretaker the provision of empathically attuned challenges involving an unmet want or need that the child is ultimately able to succeed in acquiring. Central to this growth-enhancing process is the child's experience of **manageable** frustration and their ultimate acquisition of a desired outcome. Critical to the caretaker's ability to provide experiences of optimal frustration is their empathic attunement to both the level of frustration tolerable (without activating debilitating emotional reactions) as well as the child's available resources to acquire the frustrated want or need.

It is relatively intuitive how experiences of optimal frustration serve to promote feelings of competency, yet its association with attachment might seem less clear. This connection occurs in the child's movement from full dependency on the caretaker's direct care, to an evolving sense of competency linked to the caretaker's well-calibrated challenges and the child's awareness of the caretaker's role and presence in these experiences. In other words, the child's emotional memory of the *optimally frustrating caretaker* evokes feelings of self-efficacy and competency giving this attachment memory the power to support feelings of safety and self-acceptance.

In illustrating the concept of optimal frustration, Kohut offers the example of the game of peek-a-boo, played between a mother and infant, beginning with the infant joyfully basking in his mother's loving gaze, then confronted with frustration as she hides her face. The mother's withdrawal of the desired attention creates frustration for the child, exacerbated by the child's limited developmental abilities in object constancy. At this point, the mother's capacity for attunement and her response to her child's frustration will determine the developmental impact of the experience. The following are possible outcomes, which result in promoting self-efficacy optimal frustration, growth and associated attachment, or enfeebling *under*-frustration or *over*-frustration, both of which undermine healthy attachment.

Just right or "optimal" frustration in the game of peek-a-boo

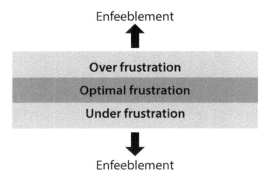

Figure 5.1 Optimal (just right) frustration in the game of peek-a-boo

Optimal frustration in the game of peek-a-boo is achieved as the infant's mother hides her face, yet empathically monitors and responds to her child's frustration in the game (see Figure 5.1). When the game is played well, the child's mother accurately reads his cues in a manner that allows her to rejoin him at a point just prior to his becoming overwhelmed and upset by their separation. By reading the child's cues and allowing him to experience frustration at a degree that he is ultimately able to manage, his mother provides an opportunity to both increase his faith in her ability to understand and meet his need, as well as experience his own felt competency. He also gains a critically important positive association between the memory of his mother and experiences of competency. In time, this felt association between mom and self-efficacy allows thoughts and memories of mom to support the child in feeling safe, confident and capable of persevering in the face of frustration even when mom is not present.

Too much frustration in the game of peek-a-boo

Should the infant's mother lack empathetic attunement and the ability to attend to the child's escalating frustration in the game, the outcome will be negative. This occurs when mom keeps her face covered until the little one is undone by the frustration of her *disappearance*, as marked by agitation. He will move from an initial sense of mild frustration to a state of high anxiety and feelings of being overwhelmed—as evidenced by tears and emotional distress. Since he has been overly frustrated and unable to effectively manage this experience, it will negatively impact his faith in both himself and his caretaker as well as his ability to utilize the emotional memory of the mother to soothe himself and promote perseverance in the face of challenge. Experiential backgrounds with consistent patterns of caretaker over-frustration are characterized by poor attunement, deprivation, neglect and abuse, and may include any of the following:

- Severe poverty, where the lack of basic resources often overwhelms the child with the fact that his primary needs (e.g. food, shelter, protection from danger) are not consistently addressed.

- Parental incompetence due to intellectual disability or mental illness, where the incompetence negatively impacts both the parent's attunement and ability to meet needs.

- The parent's need for the child to demonstrate unobtainable consistently high achievement and autonomy, resulting in limited attunement and ability to respond appropriately to the child's limitations and vulnerability.

- Indifferent, neglectful, abusive or sadistic parenting, where attunement to and investment in the child's development and well-being are significantly limited.

- An extremely insecure, anxious, egocentric or narcissistic parent who is limited in their perception beyond their own overwhelming needs. Their child's needs are attended to only inadvertently in meeting the caretaker's own needs.

Too little frustration in the game of peek-a-boo

It is easy to understand intuitively how the pattern of being consistently over-frustrated, and the consequent insecurity, would decrease a child's ability to form trusting, useful relationships. It is less intuitive, though just as true, that a child who is consistently under-frustrated is subject to the same negative outcome. Under-frustration occurs with a child who is developing within an environment that is hyper-alert and over-responsive to his frustration. In such an environment, the child is ultimately enfeebled by the lack of opportunity to grow in his sense of competency through managing appropriately measured challenges. A child raised within an over-attentive environment does not have the opportunity to develop an association between his caretaker and feelings of his own competency, therefore is unable to use the emotional memory of the caretaker to elicit a soothing faith in his own competency or adaptive skills. Common backgrounds wherein a child experiences over-attunement or too little frustration include:

- A child with a serious and/or chronic medical condition (e.g. asthma, cancer), where the caretaker over-compensates for the child's difficult reality by over-attending to virtually any expression of frustration.

- A child raised by a caretaker who cannot tolerate the child's expression of frustration in that it triggers the caretaker's own painful affect, therefore the caretaker works diligently to protect both the child and himself from the pain associated with the child's frustration.

- A child whose caretaker has a special investment in the child's life that demands that the child not experience any negative emotion. A common example of this situation is the profound commitment of a caretaker from an abusive childhood who attempts to work through his own early experience by providing a totally distinct experience for his child—hyper-vigilantly protecting him from any degree of negative emotion.

- A child who is raised by a caretaker who, for a multitude of possible reasons, is afraid of the child's anger, therefore setting the stage for the caretaker to over-attend to the child in the hope of avoiding any disappointment or frustration that might elicit anger from the child.

Vacillation between too much and too little frustration

Unfortunately, it is a relatively common pattern of caretaking to alternate between over-frustrating and under-frustrating a child, a pattern just as debilitating to the child as is consistent over- or under-frustration. Their general sense of competency and development of useful relationships are compromised by the added anxiety of the unpredictability of the parental response. Common backgrounds associated with unpredictable alternation between over-frustration and under-frustration include:

- An alcoholic or drug-dependent caretaker whose interactive style is inconsistent and contingent upon the level of intoxication, withdrawal or sense of remorse for previous behavior.

- Parents who have a highly contentious relationship, which often results in a split in which one parent consistently over-frustrates and the other consistently under-frustrates the child.

- Parents who are generally unavailable, yet periodically provide brief, highly focused periods of overindulgence (under-frustration).

Unfortunately, regardless of whether a child is subjected to extensive experiences of under-frustration, over-frustration or vacillation between the two, the outcome is largely negative. The result of this inadequate exposure to "optimal frustration" is a child whose insecurities and adaptive struggles are often linked to a lack of faith in the competency of both their caretaker and themselves. This experience directly impacts the child's openness and attitude towards relationships ("Have I experienced people as helping me feel better or worse about myself?") and their ability to remain emotionally regulated and persevering in the face of frustration or challenge.

Optimal frustration

A child's capacity and range for tolerating frustration or challenge and continuing to function adaptively can be represented graphically (see Figure 5.1) as the band of *optimal frustration* lying between *under-* and *over-frustration*. For children who are emotionally resilient, generally associated with secure attachments and caretakers able to consistently provide experiences within their range of optimal frustration, this band is relatively wide.

As a function of the width of this band, the child's movement towards being undone by frustration is generally gradual and marked by overt signs. These markers might include the child's outward expression of mounting frustration through actions such as asking for help, restlessness or mild whining. These more resilient children with relatively broad bands of optimal frustration afford their caretakers opportunity to safeguard their success by the provision of support, or the adjusting of expectations.

This opportunity for the attuned caretaker to intervene, supporting a positive outcome, greatly enhances the child's potential to experience themselves as successful, each time strengthening their fundamental sense of competency so essential to the effective management of frustration or challenge. This creates a situation where the *rich get richer*. In other words, those children offered consistent experiences of *optimal frustration* become less and less reactive to frustration or challenge and more and more able to persevere in the face of challenge, affording them more and more growth-enhancing experiences of *optimal frustration*.

Unfortunately, few children served within an intensive treatment program arrive with broad bands of *optimal frustration*. The children in these settings seem to transition from under-frustration to over-frustration with seemingly no time spent within the band of optimal frustration. For these children, virtually any degree of frustration seems to elicit either a debilitating emotional eruption or a shutting down. For these unfortunate children, and the adults charged to help them, life seems to swing between over- and under-frustration with few experiences of growth-enhancing optimal frustration. The experience of these children is dominated by apprehension and the avoidance of challenge, and an ever-expanding sense of themselves as less than others. These children too often live within a self-reinforcing loop of negative expectation and negative outcome, as their caretakers struggle day in and out to find the right challenge to afford them a distinctly positive experience of themselves.

Further complicating work with these less resilient children (as if this is needed) is the fact that a child's range of optimal frustration is a moving target, one day able to tolerate and effectively manage a challenge and the next day unable to manage the same challenge. These fluctuations are associated with a variety of factors, ranging from the child's health, to struggles occurring earlier in the day, to effectiveness of medication, to sleep the night before, to hunger, and so on.

The critical importance of providing a struggling and/or highly reactive child with experiences of optimal frustration, and the fact that challenges that fall within this range differ dramatically from child to child and moment to moment, demands of clinical caretakers exceptional attunement. For those children with whom we are unable to hit this critical range of challenge, it predicts a narrowing band of frustration tolerance and an associated downward spiral in sense of self and faith in caretakers.

The complicated demand on clinical caretakers to provide these less resilient children with experiences of optimal frustration requires a high degree of empathic attunement and flexibility. For this group of children and adolescents, one-size-fits-all expectations (e.g. academic, behavioral, relational) will almost assuredly result in far more negative outcomes than positive. A variety of interventions from meditation to medication may be helpful in quieting a child's central nervous system, keeping them in the game as they confront challenge or frustration long enough to discover competency. In the final analysis, however, it will be the skilled, attuned and attached caretaker who will be able to structure challenges and offer support in a manner that results in growth and the broadening of the band for optimal frustration.

As with all attachment-enhancing caretaker–child interactions, the provision of *optimal frustration* is tied to the caretaker's ability to approach the child with PACE. This stance affords the caretaker the empathic insight needed to know the child's capacities and the ability to support the child's functioning. Whether in the context of academic instruction, such as learning long division within a school setting, or acceptance of a behavioral limit within an inpatient psychiatry unit, it is the caretaker's obligation to assess the child's capacity to manage the challenge and provide needed support to promote a successful outcome.

From time to time, all caretakers experience failure in their efforts to provide experiences of optimal frustration. Episodic failure to optimally challenge a child is inevitable and requires nothing more of the clinical caretaker than effort to repair the relationship and recalibrate the challenge. Chronic operation outside the range of optimal frustration, generally marked by a child's meltdown or shutting down, however, demands a more in-depth analysis of the variables contributing to the missed mark. As discussed in the section above on empathy, a caretaker's consistent missing of this range speaks to an underlying dynamic blocking necessary empathy for attuning to the child's capacities and their need and best avenue for support.

Even the most empathically attuned and skilled clinical caretaker will from time to time miss the mark concerning a child's range of optimal frustration. When the caretaker sees the child shut down or become dysregulated, this moment demands a PACE-informed intervention of co-regulation of the child's emotions. In this situation, the child needs us to recognize their dilemma as quickly as possible, yet not react so soon that they are not afforded the opportunity to attempt to use their own resources. It should be noted, however, that in the clinical setting, when needing to choose between watching a child struggle to the point of unraveling vs. possibly intervening too soon, it is better to offer support. Over-challenge and failure in emotionally vulnerable children tends to be far more problematic with respect to emotional and relational growth than under-challenge. In the long run, both serve to enfeeble children if chronic, but episodic over-challenge has a far more powerfully negative impact than episodic under-challenge in more vulnerable children and adolescents.

In contemporary culture, the concept of "enabling" by under-challenging, or over-supporting a child has taken hold in many clinical settings and caretakers' thinking. Unfortunately, the notion that *under-challenging* a child (or anyone, for that matter) does them a grave disservice is a useful perspective only when balanced against the often more acute and problematic outcome with over-challenging. From time to time I have seen clinical caretakers, as a function of frustration or anger, step back and let a child unravel, disregarding any obligation to protect the child from this enfeebling experience. There are also clinical caretakers who hold such a strong ideological perspective on the importance of self-reliance that it sets the stage for their withholding of needed support to a struggling child. This is one of the many places where good clinical supervision can help a staff member understand themselves in a manner that frees them to more effectively respond to the needs of those they serve.

Conclusion on optimal frustration

In no way do I wish to suggest that accurately reading a child's needs and cues with respect to *optimal frustration* is an easy task. This range of challenge is a moving target demanding recalibration and careful adjustment from child to child and moment to moment. This challenging task, as much as any part of caretaking, demands empathic attunement, compassion and wisdom.

When dealing with a struggling child who is not well known or easy to read, the situation is similar to finding an individual with diabetes who is struggling with consciousness, a condition that could be related to their having either too much or too little sugar in their blood: **always** give them sugar. The long-term impact of high blood sugar is not good; however, the short-term impact of low blood sugar can be acutely lethal. In short, when a child is struggling and you are in doubt as to whether they are being over- or under-challenged, "give them some sugar" by reducing the challenge.

Connect–tear–repair

The critical development and strengthening of relational attachments, whether within the family or treatment setting, follows a process of *connect–tear–repair* (tear as in torn) analogous to that of muscle fiber. In the context of relational connection, it is inevitable that interpersonal misattunement and/or disappointments will evolve, challenging connection. Regardless of whether these relational injuries are intentional, rational or imagined, they are experienced as painful and disruptive to the security of the bond. Small injuries, such as a clinical caretaker forgetting to call a patient by their newly chosen name, to larger injuries, such as a staff member openly expressing angry and frustrated feelings with a child, result in relational *tears* requiring healing or *repair* if the attachment is to be safeguarded.

With each successful repair following a tear, a child's faith in the strength of the relationship grows. This is not to suggest that intentional, profound or chronic tears are supportive to attachment; for tears of this nature often remain unrepaired due to the child's inability to drop their guard adequately to allow for relational healing. Nonetheless, the healing from more normative relational tears and the re-establishing of connection serves to strengthen relationships in a manner allowing for future relational challenges to be less likely to tear so deeply. Again, like muscle tissue that strengthens as a result of exercise that tears the tissues at a level that does not deeply injure it, attachments are made stronger through the repeated healing of inevitable minor relational tears.

There are relatively few *absolutes* demanded of caretakers in their effort to support a child's secure attachment; however, the caretaker's *absolute responsibility* to assure a relational repair following a tear cannot be overstated. Regardless of the culpability, or the accuracy or coherency of a child's attribution of relational injury, it is the caretaker's responsibility to assure repair when the child has experienced a tear. The message in the repair is not, "You were right, I was wrong" (unless this is the case), or that what the child did was OK or appropriate (if it was not); rather, the message is, "Our relationship is more important than anything else." As a caretaker maintains the PACE stance even (or maybe particularly) in setting appropriate behavior limits and consequences, the process of tear repair is approachable in even the most difficult of situations.

Should the caretaker choose to wait for the child to come to the table with an act of contrition to open the door to reconnection, things are not likely to go well. Again, this is not to suggest that the caretaker is to take all responsibility for a tear, but they **are** to take responsibility for the repair.

The caretaker's pursuit of a repair with a child who seems to have initiated or been responsible for the *tear* is sometimes counterintuitive, often involving a caretaker attitude of, "Why should I be the one trying to make things better, I am not the one who created the tear?" The answer to this question is, "Because it is your job as a clinical caretaker to give the child what they need to allow for growth and development." Regardless of who caused the tear, it must fall on the caretaker's shoulders to seek means for the repair or else both the relationship and the child's development and healing are in peril.

The process of overcoming the often counterintuitive need to pursue relational repair with a child (or adolescent) when not responsible for the tear is an important clinical caretaking (if not general relational) skill. This skill often centers upon the caretaker learning to approach the issue in a manner that is empathic and neutral in its attribution of the tear to the child or the caretaker. This might take the form of the clinical caretaker saying something like, "When I told you that you couldn't go outside you were so mad and sad that next thing you knew you were hitting me." Or, "When I told you that it was time to turn off your computer game you were just about to win that level and you just couldn't pull yourself away, and before we knew it we were in a tussle with one another." The process of identifying the dynamic that drove a problematic exchange and an associated tear in a neutral and accepting manner is an important first step. The next step is the expression of sadness that neither person seemed to know how to not have things fall apart from that point. In no way does this process require the caretaker to step back from the enforcement of appropriate consequences for the child's behavior, but it does require their capacity to empathize and support the child in managing their negative reaction to the consequences (e.g. "I know that you hate the rule that says you lose your game for a day when you don't get off it when asked. I also know that sometimes it is really hard to turn the game off—I really am sorry about this").

Clinical caretakers who understand and respond well to the demand to repair relational tears provide children the necessary security to tolerate difficult relational dynamics without undue fear or anxiety. This security supports children in maintaining an emotionally regulated state, affording them access to higher-level cognitive capacities even in the face of relational stress.

Chapter 6

UNDERSTANDING AND USING CO-REGULATION OF EMOTION AS A PRECURSOR TO SELF-REGULATION

Perhaps as important as any aspect of development addressed within the clinical setting is the provision of support to the child's evolving capacity to regulate emotions. In the absence of this capacity, they are left to manage life's challenges with a brain easily over-activated to the point of agitation and associated diminished higher-level thinking. How difficult a life, if when most needing to think clearly, higher-level thought is shut down and the lower brain runs the show offering little more than fight, flight or freeze responses. This is a reality described by Siegel and Bryson in *The Whole Brain Child* (2012) as flipping one's lid, effectively shifting from thought and action directed by the upper brain to control by the lower, more primitive brain.

During early childhood we expect and accept the simple or primitive fight, flight or freeze response as the child's only avenue for adaptation to stress or challenge. Yet with maturation the need for the child to down-regulate these primitive reactions and access higher-level thinking is needed and expected. In recognizing that some children make this developmental leap with relative ease while others struggle immensely, we are left to question the cause for this developmental variance.

This variance in the capacity to regulate emotion has been attributed to many factors including temperament, brain chemistry, culture and experience. There is no doubt that all of these play some role in the development of the capacity to regulate emotion, but much research now suggests that none of these is as central or core as a child's access to caretakers who know how to teach emotional self-regulation through the process of *co-regulation.*

Emotional co-regulation

Emotional co-regulation is understood as the stepping-stone to self-regulation, involving a process in which a child learns to regulate their reaction to powerful emotion through repeated interactions with caretakers able to attune, accept and empathically join the child in quieting powerful emotions.

As with a parent responding to an upset infant, the process begins with a non-verbal reflection of a parallel affect. This involves the caretaker assuming an exaggerated sad facial expression, picking up the crying child and saying something like, "Oh,...what's the matter, little guy?" in a regulated but concerned voice.

The matching of the child's affective expression is an essential aspect of connecting with the upset child or adolescent, as with the infant. This is sometimes described as the caretaker matching the *vitality* (Stern 1985) of the child's affective state while maintaining a well-regulated internal emotional state themselves. It is from this starting point that the process of co-regulation almost always begins, as the caretaker expresses awareness and acceptance of the child's emotions and the ability to be with them in an attuned, yet calm (regulated) manner.

It is from this point of connection with the child's activated emotional state that the process unfolds, preceding from the inherent comfort of shared affect, to the caretaker's offering of a pathway back to higher-brain functioning through the development of a story (narrative) about what has happened and eventually a plan for moving forward.

Again, co-regulation always begins with the matching of the child's affect, not their emotional state. This matching is largely through non-verbal communication and tracks with the child whether up or down with respect to affect, while the caretaker remains emotionally regulated. This may take the form of reflecting everything from the child's affective excitement about arrival at the amusement park entrance, to his sadness in loss of a loved stuffed animal, always trying to match affect and not getting pulled too far into the content of the child's words or efforts at problem solving.

As simple as this process may sound, the reality of carrying it forward may be complicated by a number of factors. These include the caretaker's lack of awareness of the child's emotional state, lack of acceptance of the validity or acceptability of the child's reaction, the child's unwillingness to allow the caretaker in, conflicting demands in the environment (e.g. other upset kids) and the caretaker's own emerging emotional dysregulation.

Example of co-regulation in a typical daily event

The following scenario is offered as an illustration of co-regulation in the context of a typical daily event. Much of this section is discussed in the broad context of caretaking in that there is no difference between good general caretaking and effective clinical caretaking.

A six-year-old boy is outside with his dad learning to ride his bike without training wheels. All is going well until he begins to get the hang of it and speeds off beyond his dad's reach. Initially riding well, but then feeling insecure and looking for Dad's hand to steady the bike, he recognizes Dad is no longer beside him, panics and crashes to the pavement, scraping his knee. Dad runs up to the crash site, bends down to the child, and the following co-regulating scenario plays out as the dad helps the upset child regain equilibrium after the upheaval associated with the fall and injury.

> Child, sobbing, and looking at Dad: "My knee!!! Why did you let go of me???? You know I don't know how to ride without training wheels!!! I hate that stupid bike and you let me get hurt!!! I'm probably going to need stitches and it is really going to hurt and it's your fault!!!"

> Dad, kneeling beside the sobbing child, gently touching his back and assuming a caring facial expression: "Oh, look at that knee, I'm so sorry that you fell!! That looks like it really hurts!!...How about we go get it cleaned up and I will grab your bike and put it in the garage for now?"

> Child: "No!! I'm not going to get stitches, I hate that stupid bike, and you let me get hurt!!! Leave me alone!!!"

Dad: "Buddy, I am so sorry that I wasn't there to catch you when you started to fall and that your knee hurts so badly! But I don't think we need to go to the doctor's."

Child: "Why did you let me go????"

Dad: "Oh, buddy! I wish I wouldn't have, but you were riding so well and so fast I didn't think you would crash. I guess I forgot that this is all so new to you and that even though you were doing great, you had never ridden alone. I am really sorry! How about I go get a wash cloth and band aid and that we fix that knee?"

Child: "NO, it's going to KILL!!!"

Dad: "You're right, buddy, it probably will hurt, but just for a second and then it will start to heal—and I also know that you are a really brave guy. Remember last week when you got your measles shot at the doctor's…you were so brave!"

Child: "Yeah, Emily [little sister] cried for an hour before and after the stupid shot. She's not brave at all!"

Dad, laughing lightly: "No, she was not very brave, was she?…I know that your knee really hurts!! But I am wondering if you noticed how far and fast you went on your bike before that really scary crash?"

Child: "Yeah, I was really going fast, wasn't I? And didn't even know that I was doing it ALL BY MYSELF! I bet Emily won't be able to do that when she's my age, she is such a chicken."

Dad: "I don't know, we'll see, but I do know that you were really learning to ride on your own so quickly!"

Child: "Yeah, I am really good at stuff like riding bikes. Dad, can we fix my knee and do some more riding?"

Dad: "I think that would be great, if you are up for it. This time I promise to stay a little closer until you have had more practice… Let's go in and get that knee fixed up, and maybe grab a snack before we come back out. How does that sound?"

Child: "Good, I want to show Emily my knee and how brave I am compared to her!"

Dad: "I guess that is what big brothers do, let's go!"

In this illustration the dad starts by matching affect with his upset son, makes a relational repair (apologizing for letting go of the bike) and eases his son to a regulated state. Although the making of a repair is not always necessary in a co-regulating exchange, it often becomes a part of the process, particularly if the child's dysregulation is in response to something the caretaker has done, including the setting of behavioral limits or a consequence provided by the caretaker.

This common aspect of the co-regulating process is often difficult, as the child turns their upset or negative affect in the direction of the very caretaker attempting to help them. In these moments, the caretaker must have the presence of mind to avoid correcting the child's perception or defending themselves. This is not to suggest that the clinical caretaker or any other agree with the child's misperception if fully inaccurate; it is, however, to suggest largely ignoring the accusation and calmly reflecting the child's perception (acceptance) until the child is regulated. In other words, the caretaker making every effort to accept the child's perception of an event even when it is quite different from their own.

Unreasonable attributions and accepting responses

In the bike accident story the dad was an *accessory to the crime* by letting go of the bike. Making the relational repair by saying, "I'm sorry," was relatively easy. A child's attribution of responsibility to the caretaker is often much more far-fetched and difficult to accept, however (e.g. "You brought me my meds late because you wanted me to flip out and get restricted to the unit"); nonetheless, acceptance is critical within the moment.

Again, there are no significant differences between what is needed within a clinical caretaker–child dynamic and a positive parent–child dynamic. In many respects, our clinical work is an effort to *reparent* the children we serve with greater attunement, wisdom, insight and compassion than they have had access to in their earlier life.

Note: Difficult to present in text, but **absolutely critical** to the effectiveness of an effort to help a child "feel felt" in the initial step of the co-regulation process are *the clinical caretaker's non-verbal expressions.* If the child does not perceive the caretaker's words as congruent with their non-verbal expressions (e.g. tone of voice), a sense of acceptance or "feeling felt" will **not** occur for the child.

As Siegel and Bryson (2012) speak of in *The Whole Brain Child,* it is essential to meet an upset child *right brain to right brain,* the child's dysregulated right brain to the caretaker's regulated and empathic right brain, remembering always that the language of the right brain is our non-verbals and they are processed 10 to 50 times faster than our words. Therefore, before a word is processed the child is reacting, either positively or negatively, to the messages being sent by our facial expressions, tone of voice and body.

Examples of unreasonable child attributions and associated accepting responses

The non-verbals in these expressions are critical:

> » Child: "None of my friends can come over to play because you painted my room blue and they hate it!"
>
> Caretaker: "Oh, buddy, I am sorry none of your friends can come over, I know how much you like to play with them and how sad you get when they can't. If the new color of your room has anything to do with this, I am really sorry!"

> » Child: "You like taking away my freedom and keeping me here in the hospital even though it is your fault that I am here in the first place!"
>
> Caretaker: "I know you are upset about being here and that makes sense to me. It must be so hard feeling like we are keeping you in here against your wishes because we don't care."

> » Child: "You hate me and that's why you don't let me go down to the cafeteria."
>
> Caretaker: "Here you are in the hospital where you don't want to be and your life is being controlled by someone you think hates you. That has to suck—I am really sorry it feels like this!"

>   Child: "You said I was supposed to be able to go off the unit after I was here for a day and now you say I can't just because you found that piece of glass hidden in my pillow—all you ever do is lie to kids then lock them in seclusion. You are such a liar!!"

Caretaker: "I get why it feels that way and I am sorry this is so hard and confusing. This is a hard place to be and there are so many rules to learn and it seems like we are often changing them from minute to minute."

These kinds of responses are not intuitive and often take considerable restraint, yet when done well serve to pull the interaction away from an unproductive and increasingly agitated struggle. It is critical to remember that the caretaker's position is one of *acceptance* of the child's perception, not embracing of the perception as true.

In recommending these kinds of responses, I accept that it is common for clinical caretakers to express concern that indulging the child's misperception and allowing them to project blame onto others does not hold them accountable, or teach them more adaptive strategies. We must remember, however, that an agitated child is **not** in a position to learn. Once they are calm and again able to think clearly, a different discussion may occur; or often will not need to occur in that the child will correct their misperceptions on their own when not *pushed into the corner* by the caretaker to be more reasonable.

This process of "letting go of the rope" in the tug-of-war of defining "the truth" generally results in the caretaker being perceived as powerful and effective by both the child and themselves. As the child experiences the caretaker as not **needing** them to endorse their perspective or reality, it communicates to both the child and to the caretaker security in the caretaker's sense of self. Conversely, when a child experiences their caretaker, clinical or otherwise, as needing them to accept their perception, their thwarting of this need affords the child a sense of power, greatly undermining the caretaker's ability to be experienced as strong and comforting to the upset child.

In the final analysis, the caretaker must be perceived as wise, compassionate and powerful, if they are to be effective in supporting an upset child in calming. When a caretaker enters a power struggle with a child around issues such as the attribution of culpability for a bad moment, they are generally experienced by the child as none of the above.

Chapter 7

EXECUTIVE FUNCTIONING WEAKNESSES, ATTACHMENT AND ORGANIZATION OF THE TREATMENT MILIEU

A child's broad capacity to form and use an organized perception of their inner and outer world is largely linked to their brain's left prefrontal cortex and neurocognitive abilities referred to as *executive functioning*. This is a capacity now understood to be tied as much to the child's experiential background as genetics. It is this capacity that affords children the ability to develop accurate and useful perceptions (organizational schemas or models) for both the world around them and the world within them. This capacity plays an enormous role in a child's experience of the world and themselves as coherent and predictable.

For children with limited ability to form coherent models, or understandings of their inner and outer worlds, life is much like rowing a boat in high seas; where the unpredictable movement of both the water and the boat allow little focus aside from simply trying to stay in the boat. This results in a sense of the world around them as wholly unpredictable and the world within them as no more than a random series of thoughts, feelings and behaviors. An experience that undermines even the hope of being able to identify a desired destination or course.

For these unfortunate kids living with profoundly weak executive functioning, often associated with having grown up amidst a great deal of environmental and relational chaos, it is the treatment settings responsibility to provide a safe consistent/predictable environment marked by supportive relationships consistently reflecting back to the child the belief that they make sense in support of their development of a coherent evolving sense of self. This chapter will provide insight concerning the nature of executive functioning deficits and their management in a manner that promotes the calming of the sea, the child's development of a cohesive and coherent self, and their capacity to create and rely upon accurate perceptions of the world around them.

Making sense of the environment

The capacity to make sense of (or organize) one's environment entails the ability to separate essential from non-essential detail, the sequential nature of events and related awareness of cause and effect, all of which allow the child the critical ability to accurately predict and interpret life's unfolding realities. The child or adolescent who is unable to separate the important from the unimportant and, in turn, recognize causal and sequential patterns cannot effectively anticipate events and is forced into a subjective experience of life as largely unpredictable or governed by randomness.

Unfortunately, the experience of one's environment as random or chaotic creates a dramatic challenge to both adaptation and the critical process of emotional regulation. The individual who has experienced, and does experience, his environment as unpredictable has little choice but to adopt a highly anxious, consistent state of readiness for the unexpected and the adaptive assumption of the fight, flight or freeze response.

Many of the children who exhibit the kind of problematic behavior requiring intensive milieu-based treatment live in worlds experienced as highly or wholly unpredictable, a reality affording them few effective adaptive responses. As such, they need to either remain anxiously ready to fight, flee or freeze, or turn to another (if lucky, an attuned competent caretaker; if unlucky, someone no better organized than themselves) to rely on their schema. Sadly, for many of those in the treatment setting, allowing another to support them in organizing and/or understanding their world is something that is not readily done due to their earlier experience of others as less than helpful in this role, if not threatening and abusive.

It is normative for young children to have little in the way of useful schemas or models for their worlds, thus they need to rely heavily on adult caretakers for their safety. When such a caretaker is consistently available and competent, all goes relatively well. In the absence of a caretaker who is consistently available and able to effectively protect and meet the child's needs, however, the child develops a very limited ability to trust in the care of others and approaches relationships with either deep ambivalence or avoidance. Sadly, this dynamic leaves the child to make sense of their world on their own and to largely fend for themselves with little idea as to how to do so. For these children, the world seems chaotic and unpredictable, resulting in highly anxious, reactive and maladaptive patterns of behavior.

Factors affecting a child's capacity to organize

As we attempt to understand the origins of a child's capacity to develop accurate and useful organizational schemas, we must look at the role of both nature (neurological variables) and nurture (the character of the child's past experiences), two variables we now know to be highly interrelated.

Neurocognitive profile (nature)

From a neurological perspective, limitations in the ability to organize are linked to brain-based higher-order, executive cognitive weaknesses, largely localized in the prefrontal cortex, such as experienced by children with a variety of learning disabilities, attention deficit disorder and autistic spectrum disorders. Children with these disorders are less competent than the general population in their ability to form accurate, useful models of their environments, both internal and external. As such, these children are far more likely to experience the world as governed by randomness, and to respond to this perception by adopting a highly anxious, ever-present readiness for the inevitable unexpected.

Unfortunately, a child's weakness in the capacity to organize not only occurs, as noted above, with respect to events in the external world, but also affects their ability to understand and anticipate their own inner world of perception and emotions, further complicating their adaptive functioning. To varying degrees, these children experience life as a constant encounter with anxiety associated with unpredictable and threatening forces that originate from both outside and within.

As discussed in the preceding chapter, the caretaker's empathic attunement is an important factor in a child's ability to understand and manage their own emotions, as this caretaker **accurately** identifies, labels and organizes for them the child's feelings. For a child with weak organizational capacities, the importance of an attuned and competent caretaker's consistent, empathic reflections and support cannot be overstated.

The impact on a child of functioning in emotional isolation while trying to manage the stress of a world (both internal and external) experienced as unpredictable is unquestionably devastating. It is imperative that the poorly organized child experience their caretaker as able to structure and make predictable as much of their world as possible. This fact has powerful implications for the clinical intervention and management of such children, underscoring their need for a highly predictable environment with clear expectations and consequences delivered in a manner that offers emotional support and is informed by an empathic awareness of the child's emotional state and needs.

Experiential variables (nurture)

As we attempt to understand the experiential origins of a child's organizational weaknesses and inability to form effective models or schemas of their world, we will focus most on the child's subjective experience of their lives as inconsistent and chaotic; in other words, not governed by order or patterns. It is both intuitively sound and empirically demonstrated that being raised in highly unpredictable or chaotic environments produces children who are unpracticed and weak in making sense of their worlds.

As a function of the impossibility of comprehending patterns within a chaotic environment, the child's motivation to seek order eventually erodes, resulting in the child exerting minimal effort to understand (form an organized perception of) their environment. This "surrender to chaos" often becomes generalized and so, regardless of the structure or consistency that might be available within a distinct environment, the child will fail to see or experience order.

This limited opportunity to practice (particularly during early life) in the cognitive domain of organization often leads to neurocognitive weakness in this realm. In other words, although a child may enter the world with adequate neurocognitive ability for organization, if the environment does not lend itself to being organized, the child's organizational aptitude will likely atrophy. By analogy, an animal born with normal sight but raised in total darkness eventually loses much of its capacity for sight due to the fact that the neural channels for sight have remained under-stimulated.

An additional negative and self-reinforcing dynamic with respect to organizational capacity is associated with the fact that the experience of unpredictability elevates anxiety, significantly decreasing cognitive efficiency. This creates a self-reinforcing process of environmental unpredictability, leading to heightened anxiety, in turn undermining the child's cognitive efficiency for making sense of their world (organization), leading to a greater sense of unpredictability, leading to heightened anxiety, and so on.

Common situations or dynamics that are rife with the potential to be experienced by a child as impossible to organize include:

- life with an alcoholic or drug-addicted parent, where the parent's response to the child is contingent upon variables such as the parent's level of intoxication or withdrawal that the child cannot understand or assess

- life with a mentally ill parent, where non-observable, intrapsychic factors within the parent change dramatically, without explanation or notice, and profoundly impact parent–child interaction

- a life of poverty, in which families must respond to basic needs and cannot attend to higher-level issues of security or stability (e.g. a child may find themselves living in a shelter with dangerous or unstable adults to avoid freezing on the street).

Clearly, children who experienced their lives as unpredictable due to neurological and/or experiential variables ultimately show decreasing ability and motivation to even try to make sense of their worlds.

Hope for these children lies in the opportunity to be cared for by caretakers able to provide a consistent, predictable, safe and caring environment; able to support the child's management of anxiety while they learn to see the provided structure in their new lives, and allowing them to experience the boundaries associated with a well-structured life as firm, but gently padded (see the section on padded boundaries in Chapter 8).

Program challenges in work with children with weak organizational capacity

Effective work with children with weak organizational capacity demands a high level of empathic attunement to this limitation and associated emotional vulnerability. Two central factors seem to account for this challenge.

First, due to their weak capacity for organization, these children are often limited in their ability to form an organized sense of their own needs—and are equally limited in their ability to effectively communicate these needs to others. This often sets the stage for a situation where a confused caretaker looks to a confused child to tell them what the child needs. Unfortunately, almost without exception the net result of this is increased anxiety, frustration, a sense of isolation and hopelessness for both caretaker and child.

The second central factor is the challenge in achieving empathic attunement when dealing with an individual whose ability and temperament are quite different from one's own. It follows logically that those with good ability to organize, including most working within the treatment milieu, will experience difficulty in accurately perceiving and understanding the experience and perceptions of a child with significant weakness in organization whose needs are much younger than would be expected for their chronological age.

Through my experience as a consultant to many treatment milieus, I have observed one of the greatest obstacles to effective work with this population to be misinterpretation of the fundamental needs and motivations of children with weak executive functioning. This is not to suggest that clinical caretakers are indifferent concerning these needs, but rather that their stronger capacities within this area limit their understanding of the child's experience of the world. This limitation often results in an empathic miss in which caretakers provide for a child the organizational support or structure that they themselves or a more typical child might need, in turn dramatically under-supporting the child and misinterpreting confusion for obstinance.

The most common way in which children with weak organizational skills are misunderstood is in the under-estimation of their need for explicit (gentle) guidelines and structure. Frequently, staff may establish what they believe to be relatively clear guidelines and structure only to have these kids not fall into place. This is not to suggest that volitional opposition is never a factor in a child's non-compliance, but it is to say that more often than not, at the core of oppositional behavior is the child's limited understanding of expectations, limited ability to effectively read organizational cues, or an effort to gain a sense of control in a world they experience with great anxiety due to their perception of its random or chaotic nature. When executive functioning is not the root to oppositionality, there are other roots such as insecure attachment and difficulty with emotional regulation that must be understood and managed—all behavior makes sense and is driven by a need.

It is also important to recognize that children with weak organizational skills initially respond to an environment with clear structure and boundaries by stumbling and/or crashing into them and defensively challenging their existence and legitimacy. This fact often misleads caretakers to believe that the organizationally weak child rebels against structure and boundaries, when in reality it simply takes them longer to recognize and respond to structure. With time to understand and master environmental boundaries, the organizationally weak child ultimately finds great security and comfort in them.

Unfortunately, caretakers, within or outside of the clinical setting, too often respond to the seemingly relentless challenges of these kids to boundaries with frustration and relatively negative affect. This response in turn often serves to increase the child's anxiety and decrease their ability to comprehend and learn to live comfortably within these boundaries.

A note on oppositional defiant disorder

In somewhat of a digression, let me take a paragraph (or two) to rail against the inexcusable use of the diagnosis of oppositional defiant disorder (ODD), as if it explains anything more than a child's adaptive response to a life that has been in many ways unmanageable.

The "oppositional" child is exhibiting a symptom of an underlying developmental issue, and any diagnostic system or process that does not emphasize this fact is truly a disservice to the child, too often supporting a destructive sense of the child as a simple volitional pain in the ass. Sadly, this perception often leads to the management of the child's behavior in a manner parallel to the dynamics that promoted the oppositionality in the first place.

Giving a child the ODD diagnosis without clearly linking it to some combination of underlying issues such as attachment, mood or executive functioning is no more helpful than seeing a physician when ill and having him proclaim that he has found the problem: "You have a fever." The fever is always there as a manifestation of the underlying issue, as is the oppositionality; it may be critical to treat the fever, **but this is NOT enough**. We must seek to understand the underlying issue(s) and address them if we are to truly be a part of healing. Whenever a diagnosis seems to effectively stifle deeper empathic understanding and wise compassionate response, as has too often been the case with ODD, conduct disorder and borderline, we have to be very careful in its use.

Analogy to support empathic understanding of a life with limited executive functioning skills

In an effort to support clinical caretakers in the development of a greater empathic understanding of children weak in organizational skills, I offer the following two-part analogy. The first is illustrative of the experience of an individual with good organizational capacity and the second illustrates the life of someone weak in this realm.

Life as someone with good organizational capacity

A large group of adults have gathered to participate in a day-long training designed to help them in their work with students with behavioral handicaps. Early in the day, after requesting that two participants remain behind, the conference leader directs the rest of the group to a large, empty room adjacent to the meeting space. Once in the room, the leader places eight to ten volleyballs on the floor, with instructions that the participants spread themselves evenly around the perimeter of the room and distribute the balls among themselves.

The leader then provides the group with instructions to be followed when he brings in the first of the two chosen participants to rejoin the group. The group is instructed to stand quietly as the leader places the first participant, subject A, in the center of the room and walks back to the perimeter. Then, upon the leader's command, "GO!" group members who have a ball are to call out "HERE!" and one at a time throw the ball at subject A, and they are to continue this process until instructed to stop.

As subject A, for no reason comprehensible to him, finds himself in the center of a room, surrounded by strangers who are calling out and throwing balls at him, he undoubtedly will experience heightened anxiety. In all likelihood, however, he will quickly begin to form an organized perception of the situation: He will recognize the people surrounding him as fellow conference attendees and as relatively non-threatening, identify the objects being thrown at him as volleyballs, and realize a pattern in which someone calls his attention and then throws a ball in his direction.

As a result of his ability to develop an accurate and organized sense of this situation, subject A's anxiety level will remain relatively low, allowing him to think clearly and respond adaptively. This adaptive response is likely to entail turning to catch the balls as they come his way while attempting to establish a rapport with the group through the use of eye contact, humorous comments and facial expressions. Eventually, either by collecting the balls as they are thrown or through establishing a rapport that alters the behavior of the group subjecting him to this treatment, subject A will effectively manage his dilemma.

In this scenario, subject A's ability to rapidly develop an understanding (schema) for his situation allows him to respond adaptively, resulting in the lowering of his anxiety, heightening of his cognitive efficiency and an ongoing adaptive response. As a result, subject A not only manages this situation effectively, but gains reinforcement for his general sense of competency. This affirmation of subject A's competency will, in turn, serve him in future encounters with challenging situations by providing a positive expectation for his ability to manage difficult dilemmas and associated reduced anxiety to do so.

Analogous to life as a child with weak organizational capacity

This exercise unfolds in much the same way as the first, but involves the second of the pre-selected participants (Subject B) being led blindfolded to the center of the large room, after the leader has made two significant changes in his directives to the group. Unlike subject A, subject B will not be given a verbal cue before the balls are thrown, and more importantly, the lights in the room are to be turned off, making vision very limited.

After being led to the center of the room, subject B stands blind, hears the directive, "GO!" and immediately confronts a series of flying objects. Unlike subject A, who had both sight and sequential auditory cues to support him in quickly and accurately developing an organized sense of his situation, subject B is unable to develop a useful model for what is going on. Subject B's experience is characterized by an inability to determine who is surrounding him, what is being thrown, and when or from where the next projectile will come. This inability to develop a model for understanding his situation results in subject B experiencing his environment as wholly unpredictable and elicits a highly anxious sense of vulnerability that activates a fight, flight or freeze response and the assumption of a fetal position on the floor in order to escape from harm.

Subject B's response, although understandable, does little or nothing to affect his situation directly and sets the stage for him simply to endure his plight until some external factor intervenes. Unlike subject A, who actively adapted and ultimately gained affirmation of his competency through his experience, subject B must simply suffer his dilemma, experiencing increasing anxiety and decreased capacity to think or problem solve.

Ultimately, as the large group continues to pelt subject B with balls, it is likely that one of the participants will begin to feel uncomfortable with this situation. Judging the group's actions to be unfair (if not sadistic), he might attempt to protect or help subject B. As he approaches in total darkness and touches subject B on the shoulder in an effort to find and support him, however, subject B's reaction to his gesture is not likely to be an immediate expression of gratitude. Rather, it is more likely to be one of defensive aggression—

striking in the direction of the very individual who is trying to help him. Although this compassionate participant's motivation is to help subject B, it is experienced or perceived by him as simply another unpredictable threat to which he must respond defensively.

Now further complicating subject B's situation is the reaction of his potential rescuer, who set out to be helpful and in the process got whacked for his effort. If the rescuer responds with anger (an understandable yet unfortunate reaction) and either abandons the effort to help or retaliates, the plight of subject B becomes even more difficult.

Many of the children who end up in intensive treatment programs have had multiple experiences similar to that of subject B. Often unable to understand or predict much of what happens to them and around them, they remain constantly anxiously poised on the threshold of fight, flight or freeze responses and highly prone to lashing out at the very people attempting to help them.

Recognition of the difficult reality associated with a life impacted by weak executive functioning, clinical caretakers must respond with both an explicitly structured and highly predictable milieu, as well as gentle and supportive tolerance for the slow process through which these children grow to understand and operate within this structure. For this population of kids, variety is rarely the spice of life; change and transitions are difficult. Once settled into a well-understood structure and set of expectations, however, these kids often thrive and are highly reactive to variation in the structure.

In supporting children and adolescents weak in organization, it is helpful to define needed structure and predictability around four domains: *time, space, rules and expectations* and *interpersonal structure*, all of which will be discussed in detail in the following chapter, recognizing that the treatment milieu must thoughtfully consider and provide each.

Chapter 8

ATTACHMENT-INFORMED LIMIT SETTING WITHIN THE TREATMENT MILIEU

Holding on to Your Power with Compassion, Wisdom and Wiliness

As discussed in Chapter 7, the majority of the children served within intensive treatment programs present with significant overt and subtle organizational weaknesses. These weakness take the form of difficulty in attending to more than one thing at a time (split attention), relating new situations to older experience, reading environment cues, sequential organization, and memory and impulsivity (very little time between thought and action).

In focusing on *attachment-informed structure and limit setting* within the clinical setting for children with this common deficit, the following seven points are important to remember:

1. Children with weak executive functioning and the adults who care for them will encounter many difficult and frustrating moments on the path to higher adaptive functioning.

2. These children desperately need structure and predictability, but their initial response to this structure will often be to ignore, fight and push it away.

3. Organizational weakness interferes with a wide range of adaptive capacities, including the development of an organized sense of one's inner world of thoughts and feelings, resulting

in these children constantly confronting unexpected reactions from both themselves and others.

4. Much of what is experienced as "oppositional" by caretakers in dealing with these children is a function of the caretakers' lack of attunement to the child's limitations in understanding and responding to structure and cues.

5. It is not easy to maintain patience and compassion as a caretaker for children with significant executive function weaknesses; however, if a child's caretakers are not (for the most part) able to remain calm and supportive of the child in co-regulating the emotions associated with their repeated adaptive failures, their anxiety will further undermine their organizational abilities.

6. Punishment does not teach a lagging skill (Greene and Ablon 2006). Challenged boundaries by children with weak organizational skills are best interpreted as a function of a skill deficit that cannot be coherently addressed through punishment. Punishment for an incapacity promotes in children hopelessness, anger, depression and the blocking of connection with caretakers.

7. Remember that oppositional behavior is often largely rooted in organizational weakness; let go of the struggle and help the child redirect their attention and reorganize their experience.

Use and misuse of behavioral limits

Children and adolescents need appropriate behavioral limits to enable them to thrive. Limits and structure afford them a sense of the world as predictable and safe, and their caretakers as wise and powerful. Structure affords children the opportunity to make sense of both their internal and external environments and to practice adaptive skills within a world that is mostly predictable and not overwhelmingly unpredictable.

Effective limit setting within the clinical milieu is first dependent on the thoughtful discernment of which limits to set, and then on the clinically effective process of setting these limits. Both of these variables are central to a well-run milieu. Some boundaries are so unimportant, others so provocative, that thoughtful clinical management will steer around them when possible—holding the position, "This is not a mountain I want us to die on" or, "We lose some *battles* to win the *war*." This position must always be counterbalanced with our obligation to be as consistent, predictable and compassionately powerful as possible. For the clinical caretaker, attributes of empathic attunement and tolerance of ambiguity are critical.

Effective limit setting demands not only empathic attunement, but also flexibility and sometimes creativity on the part of the caretaker. First, flexibility in responding to the child's changing emotional states and associated needs for support in tolerating limits (a child may begin an encounter well regulated and quickly become undone in a manner demanding a significant shift in caretaker stance). Second, flexibility in responding differently from child to child, as well as from moment to moment with a given child. Third, flexibility in responding to changing environmental dynamics (e.g. if a child is challenging a limit in going behind the nursing station when the doctor asks him to come back there to speak with him, this is not the time to try to get the doctor to join you in setting the limit).

As much as children need limits, their innate drive for autonomy and expanding competency places them in frequent struggle with these limits. It is this inevitable struggle and the manner in which caretakers manage it that largely determines the nature of the caretaker–child relationship.

When the caretaker has the wisdom and compassion to understand and accept the child's struggle with limits, while at the same time the skill to effectively uphold them, things generally go well. If the child's resistance to limits is met by a caretaker who too readily gives in, or too rigidly and aggressively enforces the limit, however, little good will come from the experience.

A metaphor useful in our effort to establish and uphold effective limits is the idea of "padded boundaries." Children require boundaries to feel safe; however, it is important that these boundaries be established and enforced in a manner that is clear and powerful, yet as gentle as possible.

A limit can be understood as similar to a wall, strong and immovable; and should this wall be made of brick, the child's collision with it will be startling and painful and their association with the wall one of anger and fear. Conversely, if this same wall is well padded, allowing it to stand strong yet making the child's collision with it as gentle as possible, the important boundary stands, while at the same time minimizing the child's negative experience and associated defensive response of anger and resistance.

The process of "padding" a boundary is not particularly difficult if we are aware of the critical importance of this effort and are in the frame of mind to effectively do so. It generally demands little more than a gentle or PACE-like stance in our limit setting.

In this process, the caretaker must watch carefully to avoid non-verbal cues of anxiety, anger, frustration or irritation. If instead they are able to *matter-of-factly*, kindly and even playfully set limits, the child's central nervous system is far more likely to remain in a regulated and cooperative state of learning. Should they approach the child with what the child experiences as anxiety, anger, frustration or irritation, however, it will activate the child's lower brain into a problematic stance of opposition, self-protection or defensiveness. The process of setting a limit and not activating emotional reactivity and resistance (or at least as little as possible) is at the core of effective caretaking. Specific strategies and mindsets to use in the *art* of padded limit setting are discussed below.

Again, dealing with children who have encountered few limits, have been frequently overwhelmed by their environments and/or have had a great deal of inconsistent and harsh limit setting, effectively setting a limit and gaining compliance without activating emotional dysregulation is often truly challenging. This is much like the catching of a floating soap bubble, which demands as much care in how we catch it, as in catching it.

There are those among us who are intuitively gifted in this process and like the Pied Piper are remarkable in wooing children into gentle compliance. Blessed are these folks for they make our treatment milieus much quieter places. Most of us must learn this skill, however, and will have varying degrees of success due to a wide range of factors. No factor is more critical than the clinical caretaker's, often unconscious, display of non-verbal cues expressing calm, playfulness and unconditional caring and acceptance.

This initial critical step in limit setting is referred to by Dan Siegel and Tina Bryson (2014) in *No Drama Discipline* as "turning down the shark music," a reference to the ominous "da-da-da-da-da-da" in the film *Jaws* just prior to a serene scene transitioning to shark-induced mayhem. This *turning down of the shark music* involves the caretaker quieting themselves prior to setting the limit, providing no emotional foreshadowing of a stressful dynamic about to come. When caretakers are able to convey a comfortable sense that things are going to go well, even if they are fully faking it, it has an enormous impact on the child's state of mind and readiness to accept whatever follows. Anxious or activated caretakers activate anxiety and reactivity in children and adolescents.

This is in no way wishing to blame caretakers for all child reactivity, but it is to say that we often play a huge role in inadvertently triggering the very behaviors which we most struggle with within the milieu. It is also to say that when we have been unable to help a child accept a limit without their becoming *undone*, we have not supported their healing. It is inevitable that within a treatment setting from time to time we will trigger a child to the point of pronounced dysregulation. This will happen and we will need to manage it and learn from it—our goal (see the section on optimal frustration in Chapter 5) is to challenge the child's adaptive capacities, not to overwhelm them. **This is what treatment in the support of healing is all about.**

Management of a child who is completely undone may require containment (a therapeutic hold) to assure safety for the child and others, but it is important to understand that our having arrived at this moment is a reflection of some degree of treatment failure—we did not catch the bubble without causing it to burst. This is a critical moment at which to ask of ourselves and our treatment team what we need to do differently to help this youngster through tough moments without their becoming overwhelmed.

Again, this will happen from time to time in all intensive treatment programs, often more so with younger children than older, but always demanding of the treatment team a thoughtful and compassionate response to the bubble (child) that did not have the strength to avoid bursting in response to our intervention. This requires of the clinical team that they redouble their efforts at effective co-regulation and make necessary relational repair with the child following the hold.

If a child should become highly dysregulated and require some form of isolation to support safety and de-escalation, it is imperative that a caretaker (preferably a trusted caretaker) remain with the child throughout the process. When this process plays out well, the child re-establishes a sense of emotional regulation through a process of co-regulation with the clinical caretaker, the relationship is repaired and the child's psychological healing is forwarded.

> *Note:* **This model never supports the locked isolation of a child or adolescent**, for it provides no opportunity for the child's co-regulatory support and promotes a sense of abandonment and shame. Locking a highly emotionally activated child in a seclusion area without the presence of a co-regulating caretaker is **fully counter-therapeutic, if not abusive**.

If we believe that it is through co-regulation of emotion that we learn to self-regulate, the locking a child or adolescent in a room alone until they calm is like telling them, "As soon as you lower your fever I will be happy to give you an aspirin." Clearly, there are times when a caretaker's presence with an agitated child can be further activating and must be handled with thoughtfulness. Yet, however it is managed, the child must know that the caretaker is not going to leave them alone (abandon them without someone to help).

Thoughtful management of this situation may entail switching off to a different, less triggering caretaker for a period. It may require the caretaker saying, "I know it's hard to have me here right now, but you are really upset and I am not going to just leave you here alone—so I will just sit here and shut up." It could also require that the caretaker keep giving the child more space until they seem less triggered, always quietly and calmly communicating verbally with few words and non-verbally in every way possible (e.g. "I am not going to leave you here alone, I will do what I can to be here in a way that does not make it harder for you, but I am not going to just go away. You deserve to have someone here to help you through this tough moment").

Thoughtfully and compassionately managed therapeutic holds, such as those taught in Cornell University's Therapeutic Crisis Intervention (TCI), are truly "therapeutic." They respond to the individual's need for safe containment when profoundly dysregulated with attuned relational support, and ultimately repair the caretaker-child relationship when needed. TCI and the author would passionately assert that it is the effective avoidance of the need for therapeutic holds that has the greatest treatment value, yet not providing safe containment to a child desperately in need of it is also counter-therapeutic (Residential Child Care Project 2010).

Once again, identifying appropriate limits demands a relatively deep understanding of the child's needs, wants and abilities. Unfortunately, there is no simple algorithm for identifying appropriate limits in that they may differ dramatically from child to child and moment to moment. The process of identifying when and where to *draw the line* for a child must be determined by a thoughtful balance between the caretaker's awareness of the risk and opportunities and the child's capacities, sometimes needing to focus more on immediate needs (the short game) and sometimes longer-term needs (the long game).

The question of how to most effectively set a limit always leads us back to PACE, for it is through the PACE stance that we learn best how to set limits in a manner well suited for a given child. Of course, the goal is to set the limit in a manner that supports the child in remaining emotionally regulated, for in doing so we make life easier for all and support the child in learning and internalizing the limit as helpful. Ultimately, our goal is for children to set their own behavioral limits and thrive in doing so.

The profoundly important *Curiosity* and *Empathy* aspects of the PACE stance allow us to understand that one child may do best with a simple directive while another child may do better with help in understanding the directive. There is no *one-size-fits-all* approach to limit setting; however, a few general guidelines can be helpful. **It is critical to remember that there is no moment in which a child needs our empathic and emotional support more than when they are confronting a frustrating behavioral limit.**

The what and how of structure within an attachment-informed treatment milieu

As mentioned earlier, predictability and consistency (structure) in a child's life not only supports the mapping out of the world around them, but also provides them the opportunity to begin to organize their inner world of thoughts and feelings (sense of self). For as life events are experienced repeatedly, the child begins to develop an awareness of patterns of response and an evolving sense of self defined by knowing, "This is what I like, this is what I don't like, this is what hurts me, this is what makes me feel safe," and so on. In the absence of adequate repeated encounters within the environment, these clear experiences do not occur and the sense of self remains underdeveloped, relational security impeded and emotional regulation delayed.

Children without evolving stable models for the world within and around grow to experience themselves as unpredictable collections of thoughts, feelings, impulses and behaviors, many of which elicit frustration and anger from the caretakers upon whom their lives depend. These children remain ever vigilant for the unexpected, a stance characterized by an anxious readiness for the employment of the lower brain's fight, flight or freeze response. In the wake of this pervasive anxious readiness, children fall into a pattern of overreactive–maladaptive responses as their central nervous system functions much like an over-sensitive smoke detector, constantly setting off alarms in response to the toaster, annoying everyone around them while doing little of adaptive value.

As noted in the discussion of executive functioning in Chapter 7, children growing up in a highly unstructured environment eventually reach a point where their normal adaptive striving to make sense out of their lives becomes largely dormant, setting the stage for them to stumble through life as if there were no way to make sense of the world around them or within them. These kids do not see or respond to most boundaries, nor the consequences of crossing them. They live much like a blind man in a game of dodgeball.

As discussed in Chapter 7, the child's adaptive failure to organize or make sense of their world is tied to both the coherency (structure) of the child's environment and the child's neurocognitive capacities for organization. The fact is that many of the children who end up served within intensive treatment settings struggle with both of these variables: lives that have been unpredictable and brains that do not see order (structure) well even when it is present. It is also relevant to remember that life within an environment which is largely impossible to make sense of results in under-stimulating the neural channels associated with organization, in turn undermining their development.

When able to develop an accurate model or schema for their environment, a child may employ this schema in a manner which promotes both adaptive functioning and a sense of competency, which in turn reduces the debilitating anxiety associated with the anticipation of adaptive failure. When a child grows to associate a caretaker with well-suited and predictable experiences, this caretaker's presence and eventually even the memory of them affords the child a sense of safety, a coherent sense of self and an expanding sense of competency.

Our incomplete empathic understanding of the child's limitations and our lack of awareness of the discrepancy between our organizational skills and theirs is one of the largest challenges in effectively supporting children with weak executive skills. The typical clinical caretaker, with well-developed and integrated organizational skills, unconsciously reads a wide range of explicit and implicit environmental cues (structure), and as a result is prone to perceiving the environment as far more structured than the child does. To help caretakers better understand and respond to a child's need for structure, particularly a child with a weakness in organization, Stewart (2002) identifies four domains of structure, which will be discussed below: *time, space, expectations and consequences* and *interpersonal predictability.*

Time

Time as a structure or boundary to help young people gain a sense of mastery and security cannot be overstated. When we are able to help them perceive and use a temporal map (schedule) within their daily life, the benefits are many. This task involves both supporting the child in understanding the "temporal map," as well as teaching them how to gain their bearings within the schedule. The use of time as a supportive structure can be achieved in many ways, often entailing starting each day with a careful look at the calendar and schedule. This is best approached by initially orienting kids to their current place in time, through discussion of what happened yesterday or earlier that morning, and then moving on to the presentation of the schedule for today, and ending with a brief discussion of plans for tomorrow. The presentation of the day's schedule should be reviewed carefully, with as much detail as possible, paying particular attention to transition periods between activities and aspects of the schedule that fall outside of the ordinary. Schedules should be posted and referred to regularly.

This model is similar to what is typically used with children in grades K-5, a group with less, yet evolving, executive functioning. It provides an exaggerated and repeated reflection on the structure of time to support them in its internalization.

Strategies to help children to learn to rely upon time as an orienting structure include:

- When questioned by the child as to what is expected of him in a particular moment, gently refer him back to his daily schedule.

- When unexpected changes in the schedule occur, take the time to rewrite or review the balance of the day's schedule.

- Throughout the day, make numerous references to the schedule and establish a routine of providing regular notices referring to the schedule and preparing for transitions (e.g. "It's 10:30; we are halfway through our reading period," "We have five minutes until clean-up time," "We have one minute until the bell rings").

- Once an activity has been completed, note this completion and refer to the schedule to determine what lies ahead.

- Whenever possible, scheduled activities should remain within the timeframes prescribed by the schedule. There is no better way to "undo" many children with emotional regulation weaknesses than to create a schedule and then disregard it. A particularly effective means to transform an enjoyable activity into a miserable experience is to extend a designated time for an activity because it is "going well."

Although these suggestions are somewhat counterintuitive in work with older children, they remain highly supportive and helpful with children and adolescents with weak organizational skills.

Space

Structuring of space entails explicitly defining particular areas of the environment as associated with specific expectations and tasks. This structure provides two aspects of support to children. First, it breaks the environment into smaller, clearly defined regions, each with an explicit set of rules, helping the child respond to complex or ambiguous environmental cues. Second, the clear defining of a set area of the environment for the performance of a specific task allows the child to develop an unconscious association between this location and the ability to perform this task.

Although structuring the child's space can be approached from a number of different perspectives, the following are several key considerations for this task:

- Boundary points between specific areas should be explicitly marked or designated, and might take the form of either physical or symbolic markers. Examples of physical boundaries include the use of room dividers placed between work areas; or tapelines on the floor surrounding each student's desk, designating personal space. Examples of symbolic boundaries include the teacher's announcement to the class, as they enter a neighboring classroom, "Remember, we are now guests"; or when the class has an indoor recess, "When the bell rings, we will be back in class session and all rules of the classroom apply."

- Rules or expectations for each area should be made as explicit as possible and reviewed on a regular basis. If able, place these rules in writing and post them in the appropriate area. It is also helpful to use a formal assessment strategy to determine each child's awareness or understanding of the rules. Approach mastery of the rules as an academic assignment and assess mastery as you would any other content area.

- When possible, specifically designate areas for an exclusive, assigned purpose, and remove a child from an area if they are not appropriately engaged in that purpose. (If, after a reasonable effort to redirect an off-task child back on task, they are still unable to attend to expectations, excuse them from their work area to a time-out or neutral space until they are ready or able to return to the work area and function in accordance with this area's expectations.) This is done not as a form of punishment, but rather to preserve the power of the association between the specific area and the task with which it is associated. If a child spends as much time in their work area visiting with others as they do working, the power of that area to elicit working behaviors will be diminished.

Expectations and consequences (rules)

An additional important aspect of structure with critical attachment implications in work with children and adolescents is the establishment and consistent upholding of behavioral *expectations and consequences*. As a caretaker creates an environment where children know what is expected and how compliance and non-compliance are managed, it supports the child's sense of the caretaker's competency, power and predictability and in doing so makes the child feel more secure in their presence. As the caretaker thoughtfully and gently helps a child manage the often ambiguous nature of expectations and consequences, their attunement to the child's needs in this realm secures connection.

Children functioning within an environment with too little clarity around expectations and consequences experience the environment as largely governed by randomness, an experience that undermines their sense of competency and increases anxiety.

As important as expectations and consequences are to child development, it is equally important that caretakers understand the wide variance with respect to compliance present from child to child. Some children are going to quickly understand expectations and take comfort in living within them; others will be slow to understand and/or comply. This variance is associated with a wide range of factors and must be managed with compassion and wisdom on the caretaker's part. The use of PACE in the teaching and upholding of expectations and application of consequences is essential, as is acceptance of the fact that a non-compliant child is doing so for a reason; a reason that makes sense in the context of their experiences and perceptions. Few issues set the stage for misattuned caretaking like a child who is slow to understand and/or anticipate expectations and consequences. In light of this fact, tremendous care must be directed towards the wise management of non-compliance with expectations and resistance to consequences—again dictating the critical importance of PACE.

Interpersonal predictability

Of the structural dimensions most critical with regard to attachment, interpersonal structure and predictability is as important as any. This structure entails a fundamentally stable or consistent style of caretaker child interaction. Within this dimension lies a broad range of variables which play out between caretakers and children, as well as between peers. This involves interpersonal consistency around issues such as privacy, emotional intensity, personal space and expression of respect for thoughts and feelings. Greatly complicating both the caretaker's and the child's management of this domain is the fact that these factors often differ significantly from person to person (e.g. mom vs. dad, staff member to staff member) and time to time (e.g. at home vs. in public or off the unit). In light of this fact, the best we can typically offer a child is a style of interaction that is relatively consistent across caretakers and time, and the provision of support to the child in understanding differences between caretakers.

As a child encounters a caretaker or peer who is deviating significantly from the expectation, it will be helpful for the caretaker to support the child in developing a narrative or story explaining this variance. Examples of this include:

- "I am sorry, buddy, I don't feel well today and I am kind of grumpy—it is not your fault."

- "I know that Tom doesn't share his toys well with you. I think he hasn't had much practice in being with other kids—I hope he gets better at sharing."

- "Dad has had a very hard day at work and can't stop thinking about it right now. He will feel better later and you and he will be able to go play like you usually do."

- "Dr. Jones wasn't here last week and I think he is kind of overwhelmed getting caught up on things—I think if you ask him for the pass again tomorrow it might go better."

The provision of coherent, predictable structure in all of these domains (*time, space, expectations and consequences* and *interpersonal predictability*) is part of what allows a child or adolescent to gain mastery over the unpredictable aspects of everyday life. When the challenges and opportunities in our children's lives are repeatedly and consistently encountered, it affords them an evolving sense of the world as safe and their caretakers as competent in their care.

Connect, and only then direct

Recognizing that few interactions are as inherently stressful as not getting what one wants, or being told "No" (particularly when dealing with a child with relatively limited ability to regulate emotion) demands that the relationship be well tethered prior to this challenge. From Dan Siegel and Tina Bryson's text *The Whole Brain Child* (2012), the directive to always *connect* prior to *directing* is wise counsel within all of our relationships, but particularly when dealing with emotionally volatile children and adolescents.

This connection may take the form of a simple non-verbal interaction, such as a smile or a pat on the shoulder; or more complicated connections, such as asking the child to show you some aspect of the video game they are playing. A well-established connection prior to delivering a directive will not guarantee ready compliance; but like a chain used to pull a heavy object, the weaker the chain's connection, the less likely it is to hold; the better connected it is, the more likely it is to result in the desired outcome.

Examples of connect and only then direct

» "Hey, buddy, show me what your guy is doing in your game."
   "Oh that is so cool! But hey, pal, in a couple of minutes we have to turn this guy off and get ready for bed, but tomorrow morning you can get back to helping him, it is clear he is in trouble without you, those zombies mean business!"

» "What are you two guys laughing about?"
   "Maybe it is best I don't know, you could be making fun of my fashion sense again! But I don't care what you say. I think my color scheme is bold and attractive!"
   "Hey, guys, in just a minute we need to head up to school. Can you grab your stuff, please?"

» "Hi, buddy, looks like you are enjoying a nice rest on your bed! The pillow over your head lets you block out whatever it is here that you want away from—I guess it could even be me, though I can't imagine that would be the case."

"In just a minute we have to head down to your family session. If you want to keep your eyes closed as we head down there, I will guide you as if you were a blind person. I know it is kind of weird, but do you want to give it a try?"

» Gently touching the child's arm, or giving a playful poke, then saying, "I so like having a chance to hang with you buddy, you always make me smile."

"Hey, in just a minute we need to go do your vital signs. Do you want to do mine first?"

Use as few words as possible and don't offer too many warnings

Many children and adolescents, especially those with limited capacity for emotional regulation, have language-processing difficulties, particularly when agitated. This being the case, too many words from the caretaker when delivering a directive can cause the child to be confused and emotionally reactive. The use of calming, non-verbal communication such as a smile and/or relaxed posture, together with limited language, is the most effective means to gain compliance from the vast majority of children, particularly those with the cluster of needs seen in the intensive treatment setting.

Also be aware of and very careful about *machine gun directives* (rapid, successive directives). Repeated directives both overwhelm children and with each repeated statement often start the processing over again; not unlike repeatedly clicking on a loading computer link (each time you click the download starts over again). Instead, offer a single or at least limited number of requests and then give the child time to process and respond with action.

Repeated directives also suggest to the child that the caretaker does not believe in the power of their own words and authority to gain compliance; if this is the case, why should the child believe in them? Repeated directives or "nagging" becomes a subtle way in which the caretaker *gives away their power* and the child consequently feels less safe and more reactive in the caretaker's care.

One other issue also arises with repeated directives: The child intuitively learns at what point the caretaker *means business* and learns not to comply until that point arrives, whether it is with the first request, or the twenty-first. Unfortunately, with each subsequent request the caretaker's own ability for emotional regulation tends to dissolve, setting the stage for a dysregulated caretaker engaging a dysregulated or shut-down child. Never a good combination!

Express respect for the child and avoid threats

Treat the child as you would wish to be treated, not necessarily how you were treated as a child. This in no way places children and adults on the same level of authority, but it does mean that expressions such as "please" and "thanks" and at least listening to a child's perspective prior to disregarding it are absolutely critical to effective work with kids.

It is also important to realize that the use of sarcasm and threats is rarely experienced as respectful. Sarcasm is almost always felt as critical and/or passive aggressive and threats as coercive, none of which feels respectful and supportive to connection. This does not mean to suggest that it is impossible to gently and respectfully orient a child to the possible outcomes of their behavior should they take a particular course; however, they should be used sparingly as a strategy to rein in a child who is highly dysregulated, in that they almost never work.

A strategy discussed by Siegel and Bryson (2014) for parenting typically developing children that is highly useful in the clinical milieu is that of attempting to distract a child from the frustration associated with a needed limit. As the child begins to scream about the fact that they cannot have another cookie, try looking out the window with astonishment and saying, "Oh my gosh, was that a giraffe that just walked by?" With a teenager in the quiet room about to cycle back into an agitated rant, offer him, "Oh my God, look at the socks I am wearing, I hate these socks and can't see why I keep wearing them— they don't match with each other and they always fall down."

These children are now distracted by the silly, unexpected nature of the giraffe sighting, or your bizarre shift in the conversation from their plan to have all of the staff arrested to your socks—the focus has shifted, as has the momentum of the child's emotional response to the limit.

> *Note:* In using this strategy, one has to be very careful to not have the child feel as if their powerful feelings and thoughts don't matter—empathic attunement to the child in the use of this strategy is critical.

A second tremendously helpful strategy from the work of Siegel and Bryson (2014) is the simple concept of turning a "NO" into a "YES." For all of us, particularly those struggling with a deep desire for control and limited skills in emotional regulation, the word "NO" can be triggering. With this fact in mind and the wherewithal for a bit of strategic thinking, a limit can be effectively "padded" by finding a way to avoid "NO" by offering a "YES" with conditions. For example:

- "Can I go to the gym to get out some energy?"
  "Yes, we can as soon as we get your room cleaned up and I will help you."

- "I want out of here today!"
  "Yes, I think we can try to make that happen if we can get you and your mom to make it through a family meeting."

- "Can I have another juice?"
  "Yes you can, but I first have to see if there is enough for everyone."

In using this strategy, it is imperative that the child hear the word "YES" prior to the condition.

Some may fear that this kind of "coddling" will never support a child to develop the capacity to hear "NO" and manage it well; however, this is not the case in that, as is outlined in the section on optimal frustration in Chapter 5, the goal is to push the child as far as they can manage without unraveling. Saying "YES" with conditions is clearly frustrating to the child, for what they want is an unqualified "YES." When a child, particularly one with the kind of struggles that land them in an intensive treatment milieu, can handle any kind of "NO," we have provided a growth-enhancing experience of *optimal frustration*, making them more likely to manage the next encounter with "NO" with less anxiety and greater flexibility.

Every time the simple or provocatively presented "NO" triggers a child to dysregulation, we increase the likelihood of the same in their next encounter with this emotionally loaded difficult word.

Managing overtly oppositional behavior

Children enter into power struggles for many reasons, but regardless of their motivation for doing so, it is the caretaker's obligation to try to avoid these struggles when possible, using connection and empathic understanding of the child's vulnerabilities and needs (e.g. anxiety when not in control). When the struggle is unavoidable, however, it is the caretaker's responsibility to compassionately and in an emotionally regulated manner try to *win* the struggle. That said, it is also imperative that their definition and process for winning not entail *winning at any cost*, or utilizing a kamikaze strategy, leaving behind an adult who has been diminished by anger or rigidity, a child in emotional shambles and a relationship badly injured.

Dealing with a child who is in an extremely oppositional stance is not easy. Again, winning the struggle when possible is important. But this battle must be won with wisdom and compassion, avoiding getting lost in battles that play into losing the *war* of helping the child develop greater capacity for connection, emotional regulation and flexibility.

In working with these kids, a variant on the "Serenity Prayer" is helpful:

> Give me the power to win these battles when able (without destructive coercion)
>
> The patience and compassion to still express caring when I can't
>
> And the wisdom to know the difference between the two.

Kids prone to an oppositional stance can be some of the most difficult with whom we work within the clinical milieu, often leaving staff feeling extremely frustrated and powerless. The task at hand for the clinical caretaker is to define their *power* as something that the child's oppositional behavior cannot take away. The clinical caretaker must recognize that their power lies in their wisdom and compassion, not in winning a particular struggle. This wisdom affords them the opportunity largely (not always) to choose struggles they have the power to win (e.g. "I am not going to have you swearing at me" vs. "You will need to stop swearing at me before you can leave the unit"). Again, the caretaker always attempts to remember that the objective is not compliance, but rather to help the child further develop their capacity for connection, emotional regulation and flexibility.

Even though I do not fully agree with all of Ross Greene's model for *Collaborative Problem Solving* (Greene and Ablon 2006), I do believe he has laid out a highly useful and compassionate way of thinking about and responding to children and adolescents presenting with oppositional and reactive behavior. His assertion that they are always *doing the best that they can* and that underlying their difficulties is a lack of skills, I believe to be accurate and helpful; however, I do not believe that Greene pays nearly enough attention to relational capacities and the critical importance of emotional co-regulation.

Provided below are several guidelines for effective work with more oppositional children and adolescents.

Direct the child towards their oppositional behavior, framing it positively

Much of the process of stepping away from a "tug-of-war" (power struggle) with a child is associated with finding an acceptable manner for the caretaker to *let go of the rope*. When this "letting go" is presented as an acceptable outcome, as opposed to a surrendering, annoying, frustrating or saddening acceptance of their powerlessness, we have often found it to be the best option among the not so great choices. This way of managing a difficult oppositional child is not only useful in that it ends the struggle, but when done well it also expresses the caretaker's commitment to the relationship above compliance and comfort with their own authority in not seeming desperate to win a particular battle.

Examples of the strategy of letting go of the rope

» When a child refuses to do their homework at the required time:

"Sandy, I think it's probably a good idea for you to not do your homework right now. Sometimes it is just too hard to do after a long day—you and your teacher will figure out tomorrow how to manage what you weren't able to do."

» As a teen turns to walk away in the middle of a heated discussion with a staff member about something that happened earlier:

"It is fine to go, Joe, it seems that this has gotten too hard for both of us. We can sort this out later when we are not so irritated."

» A child tells her mom that she is stupid and makes her want to cut herself:

"Susy, I know I sometimes drive you crazy and that sometimes cutting seems like the only way to feel better—I hate that you hurt your body but I do understand that you are doing it to try to feel better. I also understand that I can't stop you from cutting, but if there is anything I can do to help, please let me know."

» Frustrated with his writing skills, a child begins to tear at the edge of their treatment plan worksheet:

"Buddy, I know this can be so frustrating that sometimes you just need to say this stinks and do something like tear up a worksheet. I get it, and if this is what you need to do, it is OK. Maybe it will help. Afterwards we can figure out what's next now that this worksheet is out of the way, at least for the moment."

» A child picks up a plate in the cafeteria and acts as if he is about to throw it on the ground, struggling around the directive to quickly finish eating:

"Buddy, I can see that a part of you [leaving room for the fact that the child is at least somewhat ambivalent about moving the power struggle up a notch] wants to throw that plate. I know I can't stop you and if this is what you need to do to show how angry you are, this is what you will do. It won't be the end of the world, the plate will be broken and we will eventually figure out how to get beyond this lousy moment."

> »   In the middle of a fight with her therapist about being able to
>   spend time with her abusive boyfriend (Andy), a 16-year-old girl
>   bolts for the door, saying she is leaving.
>
>   "Your parents and I hate to see you not treated well, but we
>   know there are things about Andy that we don't understand and
>   that this is not fully our decision whether you see it or not. Please
>   remember that your parents have said that no matter where you
>   go or what you do, they will love you and that you will always
>   have a home with them."

Of course, there are limits to this strategy, but this *letting go of the
rope* in an accepting and kind manner can often reset the dynamics
of the moment. Framing the child's difficult behavior as their effort
to deal with an unmanageable situation is both an accurate frame and
often emotionally soothing expression of respect for the child and the
difficulty of the situation in which they find themselves. The caretaker
is not endorsing the problem behavior as a great choice, but they are
accepting it as the best the child can muster within the moment and
having some aspect of coherency, and as something over which the
caretaker has little power.

> *Note:* Ironically, *the wise acceptance of one's powerlessness* within a
> given situation is often the most effective means of *holding on to
> one's broader base of power.* Again, not too different from the wisdom
> of the "Serenity Prayer."

Holding on to our **wisdom** when dealing with a dysregulated
oppositional child is no easy task; they make us feel so powerless. In
our embracing of that which we cannot change, however, we access
the power to do that which we can.

Do not allow yourself to seem desperate for the child's compliance (even if you are)

In accepting the importance of *holding on to our power* as a clinical caretaker
in order for a child to feel safe and secure in our care, we must not seem
desperate to gain their compliance in a given moment. A caretaker's
sense of desperation to gain compliance is generally expressed in some

combination of anger, frustration or sadness, deal making and/or the offering of escalating consequences for non-compliance.

The message that we want to convey to a child assuming an oppositional stance is that we hope for their compliance, but life will go on if it is not to be had. It is not that we are indifferent to the outcome of a given struggle, but rather that we have perspective and wisdom to know that this moment will not determine how things are in the long run (some battles are lost in the process of winning the war). Again, the embracing of the fact that you cannot force behavioral compliance is often the wisest and most powerful stance in which to respond to oppositional behavior.

One of the unconscious goals of the child in these moments is often to make the caretaker feel their powerlessness (the child's), in an effort to not be alone in this difficult emotion. A child strongly tied to this objective will too often accomplish it. Our goal is to avoid more and more dramatic efforts in doing so. The wise caretaker is able to embrace the powerlessness of the moment, while holding on to the wisdom that the difficult dynamics of the moment do not reflect or predict the bigger picture (even if we are terribly afraid that it might). In a balanced response to oppositional behavior, the caretaker both holds on to their power to help the child feel safe and conveys a gentle and essential sense of hopefulness concerning the future.

If the caretaker is desperately seeking the right reward or punishment to bring the child's behavior into compliance, the child will be driven further and further into their oppositional stance. If the goal of the stance is to render the caretaker powerless, when the caretaker moves into a process of desperately seeking leverage over the behavior it simply pushes the child's behavior forward. The effective response to the oppositional stance cannot be negotiation or threats, rather it must be power through wisdom and compassion expressed in acceptance of the true nature of the caretaker's power and powerlessness and reflection of their belief in a positive outcome at some point in the future (hope).

Examples of non-desperate responses to a child's oppositional stance

» "James, of course I don't want the vase grandma gave me broken, but if it is we will figure how to go forward. You will still be my son whom I love."

» "I know you are so angry and upset right now that throwing things is all you know how to do. In time this will pass and we will figure out what's next."

» "I know that when you feel this way you hate everything and just want others (me) to see how you feel—I get it and know that for right now you don't know what else to do but what you are doing."

These statements will not bring ready or immediate compliance inasmuch as nothing is likely to do this with a deeply dug-in child; but at the same time, they are not likely to elicit behavioral escalation and they present the caretaker as wise, compassionate and powerful. Should the child's behaviors become truly dangerous, or destructive, it may be necessary to access behavioral support from other staff, the police or a mental health crisis team. This decision is always taken to minimize danger or cost to the child and is **never** represented to the child as an effort to punish or gain control over them.

Examples of statements that may be helpful in explaining the need to bring in additional support

» "Kelly, I have asked additional staff to come in to help us keep our situation from getting worse."

» "Sammy, Dr. Jones has called the police to help this situation remain safe, not to get you in trouble or arrest you. We know you don't know what to do right now and we just want to be sure no one gets hurt while we figure this out."

» "Susy, we have asked the TCI team to come and help us make this situation less awful for you and us. We will get to the other side of this and everything will be OK."

Let go of your emotional connection to your directive, but not your emotional connection to the child

One of the most important factors in managing oppositional behavior is the caretaker's ability to distance themselves from a **need** for the child's compliance, while at the same time not distancing from the child emotionally. The caretaker's capacity to remain empathically connected to the child as they disconnect from their own frustration and powerlessness in response to the child's behavior is critical, but often far from easy.

The goal in these moments is to acknowledge the power of the child's emotions as expressed in their non-compliance, yet to reflect this behavioral stance as transient and not an expression of the child's core self as *oppositional*. It is both easy and unhelpful in the management of these kids for staff to begin to deal with oppositional behavior as a *trait*, not a *state*, and in doing so to reinforce the pattern within the child as an expression of *who they are*.

The management of oppositional behavior demands of staff the ability to seek the emotion below the behavior and to support the child in the co-regulation of these feelings. To do this, the clinical caretaker must be able to remain emotionally connected, reflecting the power of the child's emotions while at the same time staying regulated themselves. There are few situations or dynamics requiring of the clinical staff greater clinical sophistication than these.

Examples of remaining emotionally connected with the oppositional child

> » "I know you can't stand me right now and I am sorry that the stuff I feel I have to do makes you so unhappy—I hope that we can work this out down the road, but I also understand that right now you just can't get yourself to do what I am asking."

> » "Being here [hospital] is as awful a place to be as you can imagine. You are angry and scared and feel like no one understands or cares about you, so you are not going to cooperate with us—I guess I get this, but I also hope that at some point things feel better."

» "Right now thinking of killing me feels pretty good, so you are going to continue to be threatening. I can't stop you from doing this, of course I don't like this, but I think in time we will get through it."

» "I don't like it when kids get so upset and break things, but I also know that you are really angry right now and don't know what else to do; and that the more I tell you to go to the quiet room, the more angry you become. So let's just sit here for now until you feel better."

» "I get it that you don't want to and/or can't stop yourself from refusing to leave your room to go to group. I am sorry you are so stuck. I will give you some time by sitting outside your door and waiting to walk down with you. If you just can't get yourself to go, it is not the end of the world. You know the unit rules that say, 'No gym if you don't go to group,' but that is just for one day. Tomorrow will be a new day."

» "I know you are refusing to go to the family session, I know they are hard. But I also know that things have to get better there for you to be able to go home. I am trying to think of things that could make the meeting easier—would you like me to be there with you, or maybe Sally?"

Note: Please remember that one's non-verbals in the expression of empathic connection are every bit as, if not more important than our choice of words! Our non-verbals must reflect caring and compassion or our words carry no meaning – particularly for an upset or dug-in child.

Carefully use playfulness to reduce tension and as a gentle expression of confidence

The "P" of the PACE acronym can be effectively used with a child stuck within an oppositional stance, but this must be done with care. There are few forms of interaction that convey a sense of security and power as subtly and effectively as humor. In dealing with a child engaged in an oppositional stance, one must be careful to not have the child experience the humor as reflecting a lack of respect for them and/or the dynamics of the moment.

Children locked into an oppositional stance are cognitively inflexible and limited in their ability to see the situation with anything other than the narrow perspective of the moment. Gentle humor, however, often of a self-deprecating nature on the part of the caretaker, can be helpful in shifting the child's mindset. If the caretaker is able to gain a tiny bit of traction from the child in their reaction to a silly or humorous observation, the crescendo of escalation can often be disrupted. Again, however, the use of humor or playfulness in such a moment must be done carefully to avoid the child feeling that their powerful emotions are being dismissed or made fun of.

Examples of effort to use playfulness as a way to break the oppositional struggle

» As Billy picks up a vase and threatens to throw it:

Caretaker: "Billy, I can't stop you from breaking the vase, but you know how scared I am of Dr. Smith and when she finds out that I let this happen, I just may need to go into hiding."

Billy: "You won't be the one that broke the stupid f...ing vase, I will."

Caretaker: "I know, but Dr. Smith thinks you are such a good kid and will probably blame me for it."

Billy: "You are an idiot."

Caretaker: "Maybe, nonetheless, your Dr. Smith can scare the hell out of me. If you do decide to break the vase, maybe we will both need to go into the witness protection program."

» As Sandy begins to pry off the molding around the nursing station doorway as an act of opposition:

Caretaker: "I don't know if the carpenters used cheap nails to put those things up or you are unbelievably strong, you seem to have the strength in your fingers of a tree ape. Let me look at those things."

» As Harry stands in the hallway refusing to go to his room as directed:

> Caretaker: "Oh my God! I just saw how I look in your room's mirror, I look scary. No wonder you don't want to do what I am asking. I look like I just left the set of *Zombie Land*. I am sorry I get so scary looking in these tough moments."

The use of humor, particularly self-deprecating or silly humor, can be very effective in managing an oppositional struggle; however, it is important to understand that the child is likely to *pile on* to any negative comment made about themselves by the caretaker. Therefore it is important that the caretaker have the available resiliency to tolerate the child's doubling down on the caretaker's playful self-deprecation. It is also important to read the child's response to efforts at humor and, should it be negative, move on to an alternative approach—perhaps the "A," "C" or "E" of PACE.

Do not act as if you expect non-compliance

When offering a directive or setting a limit, do so with a mindset and style of interaction that suggests your belief that the child will comply. Offer the directive and then turn your attention away from the child, subtly asserting the belief that the child will comply. Not hovering over a child or adolescent following a directive, 1. gives them the time and opportunity to comply; 2. affords them some degree of freedom or agency in how to comply; and 3. again conveys the caretaker's positive belief in both themselves and the child.

Conversely, if the caretaker impatiently and intensely monitors the child's behavior following a directive, it can often elicit a greater power struggle in the child's effort to assert their own sense of empowerment. It will also increase the child's anxiety and convey the caretaker's limited faith in the power of their own words. If after a reasonable period the child is not complying with a directive, the caretaker is then forced (with PACE) to assess and address the barriers to compliance and move forward with other strategies.

Be very careful about threatening consequences to an oppositional child

There are two categories of problem associated with caretakers "threatening consequences" in the process of offering directives or limit setting. The first of these is in movement to a non-PACE-informed threatening of punishment, and the second is in the giving away of the caretaker's relational power and/or authority.

The process of simultaneously setting a limit or giving a direction and threatening a punishment is a relatively common strategy used by many caretakers (e.g. "Put the ball down or I am going to take it away," "Lower your voice, or you are going to be grounded," "If you don't stop you are going to go to your room"). Unfortunately, even though this may work relatively well with less reactive children, children within intensive treatment settings who have become somewhat indifferent to punishment will often see the threat as little more than the green light for more power struggles.

With this more reactive population, avoidance of discussion of the consequences for problem behavior is often best, coming back to it only after the situation has passed. This may appear counterintuitive but once the child is regulated and basically in compliance, the caretaker and child can discuss consequences for the earlier situation. This way of approaching problem behavior is best when used within a consistent setting where consequences are relatively well defined, understood and consistently applied.

For many children, the threatening of a consequence is experienced as related to the caretaker not having faith in the power of their relationship with the child. Unfortunately, as the caretaker is experienced in this manner, it generally becomes a self-fulfilling prophecy and indeed the relationship will not have the leverage needed to gain compliance.

Another generally ineffective strategy undermining the likelihood of a child responding well to a limit or directive centers on the caretaker's threat to involve another person in the struggle (e.g. "If you throw that ball, I will need to tell the doctor and you will lose your pass," "If you don't stop swearing, I am going to tell your mother," "If I have to stop teaching one more time due to your interruptions, I am going to send you back to the unit"). This is in no way to suggest that others should not be used in your effort to set or enforce a limit, but rather that caretakers should not **threaten** to bring in someone else to enforce the limit. This threatening to bring another individual in as an enforcer effectively says, "I have no real power, so I am going to get someone who does." This abdication of caretaker authority will generally result in the child or adolescent viewing the caretaker as less powerful, eliciting both a sense of anxiety and much greater likelihood of non-compliance. Again, caretakers who have the greatest skill in limit setting are generally those who hold on to their power with wisdom and compassion, making compliance as easy as possible, upholding the limit but doing so with as much PACE as possible.

Avoid shame-inducing messages

The way in which a caretaker conveys a message to a child is critical to the way in which it is experienced. The more positive, respectful and PACE-like the message, the more likely it is to be accepted. Communication that elicits shame is virtually never helpful, particularly in work with children with significant behavioral issues. This includes both direct criticism (e.g. "It is ridiculous that you are acting so upset about the fact that we are leaving in five minutes," "Oh, here we go again with your attitude") and one of the most common forms of *shaming*: the use of sarcasm (e.g. "I'm sure that that *really* hurt," "You are *so* mature about that stuff"). Sarcasm is often a passive aggressive jab seen as playful by the caretaker, but experienced as diminishing by the child. **In work with vulnerable populations, there is almost no place in which sarcasm is helpful, or acceptable.**

The opposite of a shame-inducing interaction is one that conveys *respect* for the child, their thoughts and feelings and the poignancy of the moment. In effectively managing oppositional behavior, we must show respect for the fact that no matter what the child is doing, in the context of their experiences and perspective it makes sense, attempting to remember Ross Greene's central message that *kids do well when they can* (Greene and Ablon 2006). When able to approach the oppositional child in this manner, we support them in self-reflection, essentially conveying, "You make sense—you can be understood," and we remain available to support them in co-regulation essential to their capacity for flexible and effective thought and adaptation to challenge.

Summary of management of oppositional behavior (OMG, these kids are hard)

Children stumble into a pattern of oppositional behavior related to a wide variety of issues. The management of this behavior is extremely trying and invariably results in caretakers feeling a very difficult sense of frustration and powerlessness. It is the wisdom and compassion (towards the child and ourselves) that ultimately determines how this behavioral pattern resolves. Recognition that the child's behavior is in some manner coherently connected to their underlying pain helps us bring the necessary emotional resources to its management. In dealing with oppositional children, it is critical to remember the need to support the child in tolerating the inherent frustration of limits. This demands of the caretaker thoughtful, non-provocative delivery of limits (padded boundaries) followed by a PACE-informed effort at supporting them in co-regulating the emotion associated with the inherent frustration of the limit.

Children presenting as oppositional are difficult and even the best of caretakers is going to significantly miss the mark from time to time. Forgiveness of ourselves, as less than perfect, ready and able to make repairs with kids when they are needed is particularly important in working with children who can pull us off of our *game* as effectively as can a bright overtly oppositional child. The wisdom, compassion and hope needed to stay focused on the *war* and not get pulled into every *battle* will be available sometimes more than others; when not accessible, the healing force of forgiveness is that on which we must rely.

It is important to realize that some of us come to the management of oppositional behavior with greater inherent capacity than others. Depending on a variety of variables discussed earlier in the text, caretakers may be more or less able to respond wisely and effectively to the oppositional child. Caretakers who have experienced inflexible, coercive and punitive caretaking in their own childhood, if not clearly understood as such, will have a very difficult time accessing a wise and effective response to oppositional behavior. Additionally, caretakers with more fragile or brittle self-esteem will struggle with the powerlessness they confront in the management of oppositional children and adolescents.

These kids tend to trigger some of our least graceful defenses and demand our humility in recognizing when we have been pulled off balance. There is no shame in finding oneself in a struggle with these children; there is, however, the need to self-reflect on our emotional responses, recognize that the child is in an even more powerless position then we are, and find a means to make our way back to wisdom and compassion. This may require our seeking support from others not drawn into the struggle as much as ourselves, stepping away from the struggle for a moment (letting go of the rope) and almost always seeking a repair with the child when able.

Chapter 9

REWRITING (HEALING) SHAME-BASED SELF-NARRATIVES WITHIN THE TREATMENT MILIEU

An introduction to the neurosciences

For the purpose of this text, a very basic understanding of a child's neurocognitive profile will be offered, dividing the brain into two broad regions: the lower or primitive brain and the upper, more developed region made up of the right and left hemispheres. Those interested in learning more about the neurosciences as they relate to adaptation and connection are encouraged to read Dan Siegel's books, *Parenting from the Inside Out* (with Mary Hartzell, 2014) and *The Whole Brain Child* (with Tina Bryson, 2012); Lou Cozolino's *The Neuroscience of Human Relationships* (2014b); and Mary Gordon's less clinical but beautifully written *Roots of Empathy* (2005).

The lower, more primitive or "reptilian" brain has as its primary responsibility basic survival, controlling factors such as respiration and heartbeat, as well as the primitive survival responses of fight, flight or freeze. These fear or threat responses activate hormones and neurotransmitters, largely shutting down much of the upper brain and directing all resources towards the lower brain's efforts to survive.

Maia Szalavitz's and Bruce Perry's (2010) review of studies looking at children with histories of chronic exposure to stress and an associated overly activated lower brain reveals significant negative impact on higher-order learning. These studies have demonstrated that the quantity and quality of information ascending from the senses up through the lower brain to the upper brain in such children, can be impaired by as much as 70 percent. Sadly, this research corresponds well with other data showing that school achievement in chronically stressed children falls approximately six months behind for each year in school. Data such as these make a compelling case for the broad negative impact of chronic and acute stress, and the importance of relational connection in that it serves as the best means by which to mitigate the impact of stress.

Understanding the exact neurocognitive mechanism of relational connection in mitigating the impact of stress is complicated, yet repeatedly shown to be both protective and healing with respect to acute and/or chronic stress. In other words, the presence in the child's life of a caretaker or caretakers able to allow the child to "feel felt" and to support them in the co-regulation of difficult emotion is both the pathway to emotional health and the pathway back from stress-related developmental struggles.

Turning to the upper brain, again in a simplistic yet helpful model, we will think of the left hemisphere of the brain as the seat of language, logic and more linear/sequential functioning, and the right as the more holistic, creative, emotional and spatial region. Although separated in our consideration, these hemispheres are profoundly connected and their integration is essential to adaptive functioning and specifically the capacity to effectively manage stress.

In understanding upper-brain functioning, it is helpful to think of the flow of neural information as largely passing up from the lower brain, to the right upper hemisphere and ultimately to the left. The right hemisphere has the more immediate, less conscious awareness of all that is going on inside and outside of the child and the left brain attempts to make coherent logical and language-based sense of all that is surfacing from the right and below.

As discussed earlier, in the language of Siegel and Bryson (2012), the *river of well-being* lies between the right-only hemispheric bank of the river characterized by *chaos* and the left-only hemispheric bank characterized by *rigidity*. Well-being, balance and optimal adaptive and emotional functioning lie in the middle of the river with the integration of right and left. This integration is characterized by the individual's ability to develop and utilize coherent stories concerning what they feel, who they are and what has happened in their lives.

In the absence of such left–right brain integration, children experience themselves and the world around them as incomprehensible and governed by randomness. This essentially leaves them unable to develop cognitive maps or schemas allowing them to predict and learn from experience, much like a tourist lost in a perilous part of a city with no map or landmarks, simply moving from place to place, anxiously ready for the unexpected.

Creating a positive self-narrative

The importance of a coherent self-narrative noted, it is also critical to recognize that an organized negative and/or hopeless narrative yields us little benefit aside from small comfort in believing we know why we are anxious and/or our lives are a mess. Self-narratives such as, "I am unlovable," "God hates me" or, "I am stupid and can't do anything right" too often become the organizing narrative in a child's effort to make sense of their lives.

Very often the children served in intensive treatment settings have developed profoundly negative self-narratives and feelings of hopelessness as they loop through an internal tape and ongoing negative experiences affirming their deficits. This process is self-reinforcing, consistently directing the child's attention towards observations of hopelessness and the self-fulfilling prophecy of negative adaptive outcomes.

Recognizing the competing need to support these children in the creation of a new, more positive self-narrative, while honoring the PACE obligation to deeply accept all thoughts, feelings and perspectives, creates a dilemma often demanding a counterintuitive manner of responding to a child's negative self-story. Unfortunately, the well-meaning process of simply challenging a child's negative self-assessment (e.g. "You're not ugly, you're beautiful," "People do like you—you just don't notice") has virtually no positive impact, more often than not simply making them feel more alone with their "truth."

This being the case, how does a caring other support a child in the critically important process of creating and/or rewriting their narrative? The answer is twofold: 1. Accept the child's truth—we need not agree with their perspective but it is necessary that we understand it, accept it and not move into a mode of trying to talk them out of their "truth" about themselves. 2. Feel with them the sadness, frustration or whatever negative emotion that accompanies their narrative. Then, without overt intention to change the child's story, support them in developing a more accurate story about why and how their narrative developed.

Example of this process of creating and/ or rewriting the child's narrative

> Child: "My mom hates me, she never comes to visit. I don't remember the last time she paid any attention to me and said anything but what a pain in the ass I am."

> Caretaker: "How hard it must be to have your mom pay so little attention to you and to feel like she doesn't even like you, or even hates you."

> Child: "She does, I don't care what anybody says, I really care and worry about her but she never thinks of me, except for what a pain it is to sometimes need to take care of me."

> Caretaker: "My guess is that you want and need the same things as most kids. Why do you think your mom thinks you are such a pain?"

> Child: "I don't know, she just says that I am never happy and that she is always needing to do something for me. She says that she deserves a life too and that I just don't seem to be growing up and learning to take care of myself like she did when she was nine."

> Caretaker: "So mom started taking care of herself when she was nine?"

> Child: "That's what she says, I don't know, I do know she hates her mom and dad. She talks about how awful they are all of the time."

> Caretaker: "So you know that your mom had to start taking care of herself well before she was ready and that she is really mad at her mom and dad. Her life sounds kind of like a mess and that she never saw what parents were supposed to do for their kids and she is really mad at them."

> Child: "Yeah, that is why she says I am such a spoiled brat, because I have it so much better than she did and I don't even appreciate

that I always have food in the house and that my dad isn't out in the street drunk and constantly embarrassing me."

Caretaker: "It sure sounds like your mom had a difficult childhood and that she never experienced what it was supposed to be like being a kid. Things like wanting to have your mom watch you play baseball or reading you a story at night, even though you know how to read yourself, are not things that she understands about being a normal kid because her life as a kid was all about just trying to get things like food and dealing with being embarrassed and maybe even afraid of her dad. All that stuff seems to have left your mom with no idea what a more typical kid might want and need. I am sorry that she doesn't get this stuff and leaves you feeling like she hates you. How hard it must be to feel like your mom hates you. Even if you understood why she does a lot of what she does, it would still be really hard, but at least you might know that it really wasn't your fault."

Child: "Yeah, maybe—but it still just feels sad and frustrating when I think about the way she treats me."

Caretaker: "Of course it does, and I am sorry that you have to have those feelings—how about we go play pool and try to have some fun to not think about that stuff too much?"

Child: "OK, but don't start whining when I kick your butt."

Caretaker: "No promises!"

Planting the seeds of self-work with children with limited identity development

For children struggling at an even more primitive level of self-organization, where they seem to have organized very little positive or negative self-narrative (identity), the process of helping them develop a coherent self is even more difficult and important. Children, even up through adolescence, often love to hear stories of their early life, particularly when the story seems to reflect some aspect of who the family has seen them to be. It is as if they want to hear over and over again the *mythology* of family life, trying to make sense of who they are and how they fit in.

These stories generally carry a message about the child, illustrating some key attribute such as perseverance, stubbornness, energy level, imagination, sociability, being just like dad, and so on. For children lacking in a coherent self-narrative, it is often as if they were invisible, or as if the family was so distracted by other factors that the child simply had very few consistent messages about who they were that would allow them to begin to discover a consistent self based upon caretaker reflections.

These are not the children at the swimming pool repeatedly pleading, "Hey mom, watch this!", for these unfortunate children have often stopped seeking caretaker reflections as to who they are and have now surrendered to flying well below the radar of caretaker attention. For these children, the effort of a more attuned caretaker to take note of their thoughts, feelings and behavior is generally met with some initial anxiety and resistance. Nonetheless, it is the attuned nurse, teacher, neighbor, grandparent, and so on, able to notice and reflect who helps these children begin to develop an all-important evolving sense of self (identity) and associated self-narrative.

This noticing and reflecting of the child's thoughts, feelings and actions takes many forms but must be relatively consistent if the child is to begin to use these observations as the framework for an evolving self. Both fortunately and unfortunately, our reflections (which are often non-verbal) both positive and negative can settle quickly into a child's evolving self-narrative. Simple positive and negative reflections such as those offered below have enormous impact on the evolving self. (Readers are encouraged to read Peter Johnston's excellent book for educators on this topic, entitled *Choice Words*, 2004.)

Positive reflections include:

- Non-verbal reflections of "seeing and knowing" the child:
    ○ a smile overtly delivered as the child enters the room
    ○ a sad expression reflected back when the child hurts themselves or experiences disappointment
    ○ shared laughter over a moment of silliness
    ○ providing the child their preferred snack

- o   knowing the child's positive and negative behavioral cues.
- Comments such as:
  - o   "Boy, do you love apples."
  - o   "You really like it when it is recess."
  - o   "You are fast and really like to run."
  - o   "You feel sad when you see others feel sad."
  - o   "It makes you really mad when things seem unfair."
  - o   "I love to watch you draw, you really seem to like doing it."
  - o   "When you are really tired, it is harder to do your school work."
  - o   "You really love playing with Sally."
  - o   "It seems like it makes you both excited and nervous when your mom is coming to visit."

Negative reflections either making the child feel invisible, unknown or bad about themselves include:

- Non-verbal reflections:
  - o   no acknowledgment of the child's entry into the room
  - o   a flat, affective reaction to the child's emotions
  - o   inattentiveness to the child.
- Comments such as:
  - o   "You are just too lazy to do anything that is not fun."
  - o   "You are just like your mom and that's not good."
  - o   "When you get angry, you lose control of your behavior."
  - o   "You are just going to get in trouble until you learn to listen."
  - o   "You are so selfish with new things."
  - o   "Any time we do something new, you just can't deal with it."

It is critical that caretakers make a conscious effort to support children in the development of a positive self-narrative if they are to overcome the *corrosive shame* associated with a negative self-story. Shame often drives children towards a pattern of retaliatory behavior linked to the pain and fear of being unlovable, or to retreat to a literal or figurative place of hiding. Both responses (fighting back or hiding) tragically undermine the child's access to the positive reflections needed to develop a more positive self-narrative.

It is easy to understand how the incorporation of reflections from others sets the stage to define what we look for within ourselves; and how what we look for will generally be what we see. This being the case, our language and reflections with children must be thoughtful and wise, always conveying, "You make sense and at the core of who you are is a lovable and competent kid." We must hold on to the truth that all behavior makes sense in the context of the child's conscious and unconscious thoughts, perceptions and feelings, and that their self-narrative, or lack thereof, plays an enormous role in their pattern of behavior.

Recognizing both the importance and the slow process in changing a child's self-narrative demands of clinical caretakers considerable forethought and awareness in what they reflect. Few changes are as important within a struggling child's life as is a change in their self-narrative to a perspective of hope tied to an evolving belief that, "I am both lovable and competent."

The conveying of this message in actions and words on the part of a caretaker when dealing with a difficult child is often not easy. Nonetheless, as caretakers we must find a way to love and honor the children in our care regardless of their behavior, offering unconditional positive regard for who they are, even if not for what they have done.

For some, this is approached through a more spiritual avenue in seeing the child as "a child of God"; for others, it is holding on to the fact that much of the child's behavior is pain based and therefore demanding of compassion; and for others, it is simply "their job" to love these more difficult kids. Within each of us working with challenging children we must find what keeps us on target, recognize when we are not, refrain from blaming the child, and maintain forgiveness for the child and ourselves always.

The debilitating role of core shame in the lives of the vast majority of the children and adolescents served within intensive treatment settings cannot be overstated. This shame, associated with sensing themselves as largely unlovable, undermines essential feelings of hope and openness to healing intimacy and intersubjectivity with caring others. For these children, the critical process of re-experiencing themselves positively, allowing for the rewriting of their self-narrative, is almost fully dependent on their caretaker's ability to offer a positive intersubjective reflection.

This includes the co-creation of narratives that reflect on the good, the bad and the ugly of the child's past and present experiences and behavior; stories that depict what has truly happened, but tying these events to the child's coherent inner world and in no way impacting their being lovable. This process demands of the clinical caretaker the ability to create and tell a story, without evaluation, that makes sense of the child's feelings and behaviors and conveys deep caring; a story that is compassionately (dare we say lovingly) told with story-telling affect and directs the child's attention to the evolving nature of their story and in the process softly identifying signs of growth and healing. Difficult as this may seem, in the absence of caretakers able to offer this kind of process, very little real healing can occur.

Example of co-creation of a narrative

Carlos has just come out of a therapeutic hold prompted by an effort to assault a classmate who made fun of his former girlfriend. Carlos is a large, not particularly attractive 15-year-old with a lengthy history of peer problems and episodic aggression. He and a preferred staff member are now sitting on the floor of the psychiatric unit's quiet room.

Caretaker: "That was rough—I am sorry that we ended up needing to hold you, I know you hate it when that happens."

Carlos: "Go f... yourself!"

Caretaker: "I suspect that if I were you, I would probably say the same thing to me."

Carlos: "Then why do you do this shit to kids?"

Caretaker: "I guess because it doesn't feel safe to not try to help in a situation where someone might get hurt."

Carlos: "You call that helping? Having four people hold you down just for trying to punch an asshole that just insulted the only one in your life who has loved you."

Caretaker: "I guess I get why that doesn't feel helpful to you."

Carlos: "No shit."

Caretaker: "I get what made you so angry at Jim when he made that comment."

Carlos: "Good for you, it sure didn't stop you from getting your gang of goons to hold me down."

Caretaker: "I really am sorry that it felt like that and I do understand why you want to hit Jim and why being held is so hard."

Carlos: "You don't really get it, you don't know what it was like to have Mary care about me one day and then have her break up with me for no reason the next, you don't know what it is like to have four people hold you down! You don't know shit!"

Caretaker: "You are right, I can't know what all that is like, but I can tell it is pretty awful by how it makes you feel."

Carlos: "It sucks and sometimes I just want to die, this is just too f...ing hard, life sucks."

Caretaker: "I do get that, sometimes life is so hard and unfair!"

Carlos: "Everybody thinks I am this angry, screwed-up kid and I am sick of it."

Caretaker: "I don't think about you that way, I think what you do and feel makes sense in light of how your life has been. I understand how all of the hard stuff with your family has left you feeling really alone and sometimes really angry—how could it not? *But*, I will say that even in what just happened, I see you getting some of this stuff worked out—you let us hold you without much fight and the hold was only for a minute. This is way different from before. I know that Mary was your first girlfriend and that even though you got your heart broken, which sucks, when you were going out you guys really cared about each other and you treated her with respect and kindness, and that was impressive."

Carlos: "Look what that got me, nothing! I am getting in fights and losing my gym privileges to defend a girl that doesn't even care about me anymore."

Caretaker: "Yeah, we men can be a little pathetic in that way. I tell ya, man, I have been there too."

Carlos: "So what now?"

Caretaker: "Not much. As you said, you lose your off-unit privileges for the rest of the day, but that is just what the rules say we have to do. But you are not in trouble or anything. Do you want to go see if there is a movie on the unit that we could watch? Again buddy, I get why that was so hard and you didn't handle it perfectly; but that's life. Sometimes we handle things well, sometimes not so much, but you are getting better and better at dealing with stuff like this. Let's go look at that pile of crappy movies we have around here and see if there is something we want to watch."

Chapter 10

WHAT GETS IN THE WAY OF THE ATTACHMENT-INFORMED STANCE FOR CLINICAL CARETAKERS?

Having outlined much of what is needed with respect to attachment to support healthy development and/or the process of bringing troubled children back on track, we will now turn to developing a better understanding of why we as individuals and institutions (treatment program, hospital, school) so often miss the mark in creating and maintaining an attachment-informed stance.

Not surprisingly, the factors that inhibit an individual's and/or an institution's ability to adopt and maintain a mode of operation supportive to attachment are similar and can be grouped into three broad categories: 1. a limited understanding and/or acceptance of the importance of connection to growth and healing; 2. objectives and values competing with a focus on connection; and 3. environmental stress undermining the ability to focus and attend to relational concerns.

Limited understanding of the importance of connection

The first of the factors undermining an individual's or institution's attunement to issues of connection is a simple lack of awareness of the critical importance of connection and attachment to virtually all aspects of child development. In this situation, it is not that the individual or institution is devoid of appreciation of positive relationships, but rather that they understand neither the central role of connection in promoting adaptive functioning and associated improved outcomes, nor what facilitates or undermines connection.

This relative ignorance concerning the critical importance of relationships to positive adaptive functioning is largely tied to the culture within which the individual or institution operates. Should the surrounding culture express explicitly and implicitly a value for connection and relationships through frequent acts of empathy, compassion, kindness, collaboration and consensus seeking, it is likely that these connection-enhancing factors will be well rooted within them. If these are not actively and consciously present within the surrounding culture, it is likely that they will not be present within the majority of relationships playing out within the individual's or the institution's realm.

The power of the surrounding culture to direct attention and energy towards or away from a focus on the quality and nature of relational connection is extraordinarily powerful. What we see around us and what we have been offered in the context of relationships is typically what we offer others, unless there is a conscious and clear awareness that this is not what is best, nor what we wish to offer.

A great deal of developmental psychology research has been done studying what it is that happens within families that promotes or detracts from strong relational connection and how these dynamics are passed, or **not**, from generation to generation. At the core of this research is the insight that *what successive generations do unto the next, is as has been done to them,* **unless** they are able to develop a coherent narrative that allows them to accurately understand what happened in their upbringing, how it affected them and what they wish to do differently. In other words, it is not so much what happens to us within our childhood with respect to relationships, but rather how well we understand it that determines what we pass on to those for whom we care, whether within our families or the clinical work setting.

When considering how this issue of connection and care for others plays out within institutions, there is far less research than within the family. Under a slightly different label, however, contemporary business management strategies such as *Quality Circles* and *Relationship/ Process vs. Task* models are becoming more and more mainstream. Institutions are increasingly recognizing that employee satisfaction, productivity and retention are directly related to the quality of the connections or relationships within the organization. Organizations that express caring about staff, not using them as if they are *Lego-like* and can simply be pulled in and out of work communities without attention to their relational needs, are consistently shown to be more successful. Many institutions are moving towards recognizing the importance to outcome associated with issues such as collaboration, cooperation and consensus.

If the culture around an individual or within an institution openly values relationships, this will be reflected in much of what happens within them; however, if relational connection is not a priority, attention to issues of connection is often seen as soft-minded or sentimental. As is discussed below, this perception is often organized around a set of values that supports a distinct priority, metaphorically focusing on the construction of a building's upper floors (tasks and outcomes) at the expense of attention to the foundation (relationships).

Competing objectives and values

The second of the central factors undermining an attachment-informed pattern of relating for both individuals and institutions is the holding of *objectives and values* that compete with a focus on the quality of connection. In a culture with limited tolerance for ambiguity or dialectics, there is a tendency towards polarizing thoughts, often viewing a focus on relational connection as in contrast with a focus on outcome and accountability. When families and institutions are over-focused on *outcomes* (e.g. acceptance into a first-tier college, test scores, length of stay data) attention concerning more "foundational" factors such as relational connection becomes less and less a part of our individual and institutional psyche or focus. This kind of focus inherently values expediency, as well as outcome, often pushing for the production of more and more widgets with limited attention to the emotional cost involved to the individual or institution.

As treatment settings push towards cost containment and shorter stays, opportunities for the critical relational work done in family sessions, on the playground, playing games with staff and sharing relaxed moments among others in the program become fewer and fewer.

Within the inpatient psychiatric setting, the push for rapid change of behavior to allow for discharge through the use of medication and high levels of (sometimes coercive) behavioral accountability often makes the therapeutic intervention of relational connection seem almost irrelevant. (See Chapter 11 for a more detailed discussion of this issue.)

An over-focus in the treatment milieu around issues such as *behavioral compliance, accountability, staff avoidance of "enabling"* and *support of self-reliance* often serves to limit attention to connection. In doing so, once again from an attachment-informed perspective, we are attending to the upper floors at the expense of a secure foundation. This is not to suggest that issues such as accountability and self-reliance are not important, but rather that they are best supported through relationally informed means. Unfortunately, it is quite easy to shift focus to these secondary outcomes in that they are easier to measure than are factors such as connection or relational belonging. In many respects, within our current culture we value and attend to that which we can easily measure. This cultural preoccupation with outcome measures has led to an overreliance on spurious data and outcomes.

Environmental stress

The last of the three often interrelated factors undermining an attachment-informed stance in the treatment setting is the impact of stress and hurriedness within our lives. Our rapidly moving and ever-changing culture often serves to undermine mindfulness or thoughtfulness in directing our actions, too often resulting in a limited ability to live our values or reflect our deeper intentions. Too often the simple pace at which our lives unfold sets the stage for *knee-jerk* or impulsive interactions devoid of attunement to others or the higher calling of connection.

Even though we may rely upon the food that comes from our garden to survive, should our garden be so large and demanding that we cannot effectively care for it, our harvest will be poor. Within many of our clinical institutions, too often we have so many obligations that the core task of tending the garden without stepping on the seedlings simply does not happen.

Conclusion

Looking as individuals or treatment programs at our children's needs, whether expressed in the confusing, seemingly irrational and frequently disturbing behaviors of our more complicated kids, or those of our more typical youngsters, we must do so with an eye on the critical importance of attachment. Unfortunately, outside of connected, attuned relationships with caretakers, neither the more subtle needs of our typically developing children and/or the more compelling needs of our more vulnerable children will be well met.

Within an attachment-informed stance for individuals and institutions, we must always be asking the questions, "What unmet need is expressed in this child's behavior?" and, "What can we do to help meet this need in an adaptive manner?" It is only in our answering these questions with connected and informed compassion that we will be able to effectively support development and healing for those served within our treatment settings. There are many forces that undermine our ability to hold on to and consistently apply an attachment-informed stance; nonetheless, there is ever-increasing evidence that in the absence of wise and compassionate attunement, our children will neither thrive nor heal.

Chapter 11

INSTITUTIONAL SUPPORT TO ATTACHMENT-INFORMED WORK

The critical importance of developing treatment programs that are attachment-informed is linked to recognition that a positive attachment capacity is central to functioning effectively within relationships, as is the ability to regulate emotions. The absence of these capacities results in erratic social and emotional functioning, problematic behavior and limited ability to learn.

Clearly, the broad nature of these impacts has great implications for our clinical institutions. Nonetheless, it is often the case that these institutions do relatively little to systematically address the character and nature of relationships within them. The creation of an attachment-informed institution demands far more focus on how relational values flow from the top down (the way administration treats staff, one another and ultimately how staff treat the children in their care), than on coaching children in their relational behaviors ("empathy is caught, not taught," Mary Gordon, 2005, p.40).

In light of this fact, several issues critical to the creation and maintenance of an attachment-informed program are outlined and include focus on the institution's *core values and philosophy with respect to relationships, criteria for hiring* and *staff training and supervision.* Each of these is discussed below.

Institutional core values and philosophy

An institution's core philosophy or values as expressed in a "mission statement" is a starting point in the creation of an institutional culture. Should this mission statement focus exclusively on objective, easily measurable outcomes, as opposed to less easily measured process variables, the culture is not likely to have a strong organizational foundation in its commitment to support relational variables. Similar to parents who might define their success in parenting by their children's grades or athletic achievements, objectively assessed measures of outcome are not generally linked to underlying emotional well-being and happiness. In many respects, it is the institution's ability to explicitly address fundamental issues of well-being beyond competency or productivity that will determine its attention to relational connection. This is not to disavow all commitment to easily measured outcomes, but rather to attend first to the foundational social and emotional needs of children and staff and only after this to attend to other important outcomes; again, metaphorically working to assure the strength and adequacy of the foundation prior to the more alluring focus on the upper floors of the structure.

Whether explicitly stated within a mission statement or not, the central factor determining an institution's functioning in an attachment-informed manner is the way in which administration deals with staff and staff with one another. Seemingly small factors such as administration knowing and using staff members' names and recognizing special days (e.g. birthdays, births) significantly adds to the experience of the staff feeling valued. In most respects, it is difficult to treat the children with whom we work, better than we treat one another. In an organization where staff feel **known and valued** by supervisors and peers, the impact flows down to the broad community and a culture of clinical care is far more likely to reflect a positive and healing sense of connection.

As we consider the other two variables (presented below), it is important to recognize that these apply to upper-level management as much as front-line staff. There is no such thing as a neutral exchange; our encounters with one another, particularly leadership figures, either lift staff up or push us down. Interactions, particularly with authority figures, either affirm our importance, or make staff feel invisible and unimportant. Clearly, the greater our sense of importance to the institution's mission, the greater our commitment to its fulfillment.

Criteria for hiring

A second and enormously important variable in developing and maintaining an attachment-informed school or treatment setting is the thoughtful consideration of who is brought into the organization and who is let go. Should an institution employ individuals who are not well suited to carry forward their mission, including the relational aspects of this mission, the outcome will be compromised.

There appears to be little to no research concerning the staff attributes personal histories that support a positive relational or attachment-informed institutional environment. In the absence of such data, it is reasonable to look to the wealth of research on parental attributes supportive to strong relational capacities within families. This extensive body of literature identifies two key attributes or aspects of personal history in caretakers who most effectively support secure relational connection. The first is a parent with a positive and secure attachment history within their own upbringing, and the second is a parent who may have had a complicated attachment history, yet has created a coherent attachment narrative concerning their upbringing. In other words, an adult who understands the limitations and problematic aspects of the caretaking they have received, how it should have been different and why these limitations were not linked to their own deficits or inabilities.

This is to say that to be able to promote secure attachment, it is necessary to either have had a secure attachment in one's own upbringing, or to understand what went wrong with one's care that undermined one's ability to form secure attachments.

Again, I am not aware of specific research correlating the findings of this parenting research with non-parental caretaking. Nonetheless, there is little reason to suspect that the style and quality of caretaking that promotes secure attachments in parent–child relationships would not be operative in non-parental caretaker–child relationships. Clearly, this is an area of research that should be pursued, but in the interim we are obligated to draw thoughtful inferences from associated research as we operate within our child-focused institutions.

Embracing this obligation demands hiring practices that explicitly take into consideration the attachment profile of a prospective employee. This is not the sole variable to be considered in assessing the *goodness of fit* for staff working within a child clinical setting, in that there are other core attributes, such as organizational capacity and patience, which must also be considered. Nonetheless, it is critical and too often ignored in the assessment of those being considered for positions within child treatment programs.

Too often treatment programs naïvely attempt to separate personal attributes from professional, as if impressive professional training can override problematic personal or relational backgrounds. As nice as it would be if this were the case, it simply is not. Extremely bright individuals capable of making their way through highly demanding professional training programs are no more likely to have the skillset to work effectively within a relationally focused model than those with less impressive credentials. This is not to suggest that extremely bright, academically accomplished professionals do not have relational skill sets, but simply that the one does not assure the other. Independent of healthy relational skills, staff will likely have a negative impact on clinical outcome.

In hiring for work with clinical populations of children and adolescents, temperament and relational capacity and style are as germane as exploring a prospective commercial pilot's eyesight. This being the case, it is important that administrative personnel with the responsibility for "hiring and firing" in clinical settings have both the explicit obligation to assess relational capacity and the training and tools with which to do so.

The nature and focus of staff training and supervision

Limited training and ongoing supervision of front-line clinical staff with regard to attachment-informed work is one of the most disheartening aspects of our institutional response to children with high-level clinical needs. As much as it may be accepted that effective work with children requires the capacity to connect and understand the ways in which they operate, there is remarkably little direct support to institutional caretakers on this topic. In many respects a child's need to feel cared for by their caretakers is largely taken for granted, a perceived *given* for which no real focused training or administrative attention is required. Unfortunately, particularly when caretakers are under considerable stress, needing to manage many coexisting demands and obligations (e.g. maintenance of order, paperwork, adherence to schedules), the softer yet critical work of connecting and expressing a sense of joy or appreciation in that connection is rarely the focus of training.

It is to this end that much of this text is written, directing attention towards the why and how of connection with the children under our clinical care, particularly through the tougher moments so critical to their healing. Promoting the need for focused training in the realm of relationships or attachment is not to suggest that those in need of this training are devoid of caring or relational capacity. But it is to say that this variable is so critical to our work and can so easily be subordinated to a wide range of factors that we must shift greater organizational effort to training clinical caretakers in relational connection.

As is the case with most aspects of staff supervision, it is far more desirable to provide guidance up front, as opposed to correction. This is not to suggest that adequate up-front guidance will eliminate the need for administrative correction; however, it is to say that thoughtful training regarding the core values and desired mode of operation will allow approximation of objectives far better than no training or training that is largely organized around telling staff what they have not done well. Correction of a subordinate, particularly around an issue as personal as one's *style of connection* or interaction with a child, can often elicit difficult feelings and defensiveness. When up-front and regular training minimizes the need for this type of correction, the relational tone of the organization is experienced as far more positive and supportive.

Too often in response to what seems to be a chronic sense of urgency to bring on new staff to support struggling milieus, a relatively "green" new-hire is cast into a complicated setting with virtually no real training concerning the relational aspects and challenges of this role. These new staff, often young adults, are forced to *fly by the seat of their pants*, often responding to challenging moments with no more background on how to do so than replicating the parenting they received, or the process of emulating the more senior staff who seem to have the greatest confidence in their management skills; too often not the staff member who reflects the more subtle and important attunement to relational issues.

Unfortunately, training takes time and time spent in training does not directly address the sometimes critical needs of the under-resourced treatment milieu. Nonetheless, the impact of placing inadequately trained staff into a complicated clinical setting is rarely helpful and represents an institutional commitment to expediency over competency in a manner that undermines the security of all involved.

The nature and focus of staff supervision

Initial training, ongoing supportive supervision and a self-reflective relational stance are required if an attachment-informed approach is to be effectively and consistently provided. The traditional or psychodynamic model of "clinical supervision," addressing the concepts of "transference and countertransference," closely approximates the nature of supervision useful in the promotion of an attachment-informed milieu. This model of supervision reflects a dual focus of supportive attention to didactic teaching (social, emotional and academic) and the nature and quality of the relationship between the child and caretaker.

Unfortunately, within many treatment settings there exists a kind of relational boundary within supervision that focuses on "what is being done" and not nearly as much on "what is being felt" by the staff or children. It is as if exploration of the feeling side of the work is too personal and therefore not appropriate for a professional discussion. This reluctance to focus on a staff member's thoughts and feelings concerning their work and the children they serve disallows the support and course correction often needed to maintain an attachment-informed milieu.

We all come to this highly personal work with children with strengths and weaknesses; this is a given. It is also a given that some of these weaknesses (in some cases the most critical) are going to be linked to *who we are* more so than to *what we know*. In light of this fact, it is critical that supervision be supportive, regular and able to focus on both of these domains of self (*who we are* and *what we know*). Professional supervision of this nature is more personal as it attempts to more directly address relational dynamics and sets the tone for the program's approach to supporting relationship healing.

Effective Clinical Administration Management of Frightening Episodes of Aggression and/or Assault within the Milieu

No situation is more critical with respect to staff care than when a child or caretaker is physically hurt within an interaction. In these situations, supervisory staff **must** be emotionally present and avoid in anyway being dismissive of the experience of the situation for the child or staff. There is no *one-size-fits-all* manner for the effective management of a critical incident in which someone is physically harmed, but the need for thoughtful, present involvement with the child and/or caretaker is critical. If this is not the case, if life goes on as if nothing important has happened, it places at great peril the sense of safety of all and the fundamental integrity of the treatment program. Core physical safety for all must be a central value in any program and when this value is violated there **must** be a thoughtful, compassionate and wise response. It is important that administrative staff from top to bottom offer a supportive response to anyone significantly hurt within the milieu.

Chapter 12

ATTACHMENT-INFORMED WORK WITHIN THE TREATMENT MILIEU WITH SPECIAL POPULATIONS

Four populations requiring special consideration in the application of the attachment-informed model are children and adolescents within the autistic spectrum; those with reactive attachment disorder (severe developmental trauma); those with psychotic or psychotic-like symptoms; and those who are highly narcissistically defended. The special needs of each of these categories of children are discussed below.

Autistic spectrum disorders

Children within the autistic spectrum should be thought of as falling into two broad groups with respect to attachment-informed clinical caretaking: those with average or above-average intellectual and communication skills (high-functioning autism) and those with significant cognitive deficits. In clinical caretaking of children with lower-functioning autistic spectrum disorder (ASD), the attachment-informed model should be used in spirit, but for this population applied behavioral analysis (ABA) is a touchstone. Nonetheless, the ABA model must be followed with attachment-informed wisdom and compassion, using strategies from relationship development intervention (Gutstein and Sheely 2002) and *floortime* (Greenspan and Wieder 2009), but also high-level consistency and clarity of purpose in monitoring and shaping behavior. In light of this fact, the material that follows is directed primarily towards higher-functioning ASD youngsters who would have fit within the earlier identified diagnostic category of Asperger's disorder.

For higher-functioning ASD youngsters, the basic attachment-informed model that has been presented remains useful as long as particular attention is paid to the "E" (empathy) within the PACE directive, demanding the caretaker's empathic insight into what the ASD child or adolescent perceives and needs. These perceptions and needs may be dramatically different from the caretaker's own, but empathic attunement can be accomplished and successful as the child's somewhat distinct brain and style of adaptation are thoughtfully considered.

It is beyond the scope of this text to discuss in detail the complexity and interpersonal challenges faced by high-functioning ASD children or adolescents, but it is important to understand that for these kids, both their inner world of feelings and the outer social world of their neurotypical counterparts is confusing and often frustrating.

In light of this fact, like a traveler in a distinct culture it is imperative for caretakers working with ASD children to realize that much of what they think and feel themselves may not be relevant or paralleled in the child. With these children we must step out of ourselves, using empathy and inferred knowledge of the typical ASD neurocognitive and social-emotional adaptive style to apply PACE in a manner that allows them to feel known, felt and safe in our care. The ASD youngster as much as any longs to belong, to be connected, to "feel felt," yet sadly, the distinct nature of their neurocognitive profile and our misunderstandings often undermine their ability to achieve these relational states, too often driving them into a depressive sense of relational hopelessness and associated isolation.

High-functioning ASD children are generally uncomfortable with elevated levels of overt expression of caring, or for that matter emotion in general. In many respects, these children do best when approached from a rational vs. emotional mode. For these complex and sensitive children, our empathy must help us carefully avoid our own egocentric interpretation of their needs, thoughts and feelings, for they may process and feel things very differently from us. Again, we **must** use knowledge of the ASD adaptive profile and empathy to inform us concerning the best way to understand their world and how to help them make sense of the interpersonal world around them.

The "feeling felt" aspect of attachment-informed work remains critical, but the language of this experience with the ASD child may be less emotional and more rational.

For the ASD child, the showing of curiosity about their areas of special interest may be one of the best ways to demonstrate connection. In our learning the power ratings of the different Pokémon cards, the names of the dinosaurs or details concerning their favorite insects, they can often "feel felt" in our shared appreciation for their area of interest. Not that all children do not feel connected by caretaker interest in their world, but for the ASD youngster, this avenue into connection is particularly powerful and helpful.

Children and adolescents on the autistic spectrum are often painfully aware of being different and of not being able to form supportive reciprocal relationships. These kids are often quite kind and motivated to form friendships, yet their lack of empathy and high degree of egocentricity undermines friendship formation. They often do and say things to others that reflect what **they** would want, with little ability to read the social cues or *mindscapes* of others. Sadly, this leads them to many failed relational encounters and an evolving sense of hopelessness concerning connection. Nonetheless, when these children begin to sense that others get and appreciate them, allowing them to "feel felt," it often opens critical doors to growth and higher-level functioning.

It is additionally important to note that many ASD children are highly sensitive to being different from others and with this sensitivity comes a vulnerability to feeling *made fun of.* In light of this, the use of playfulness and humor must be approached with some caution to assure that it does not elicit feelings of being teased, put down or seen in a diminished light. This is not to say that ASD children lack a sense of humor or playfulness, for most have a wonderful, somewhat off-beat sense of humor when feeling accepted, safe and secure.

Another important area of caution with respect to this population of children is apprehension concerning physical proximity with others. For many of these children, physical touch can feel very uncomfortable and extremely provocative. When approaching a situation in which touch might be an appropriate form of connection with the ASD child, it is important to seek permission and to comfortably honor their wish should they say "No." If they indicate that they do not want a hug, pat on the shoulder or handshake, it is OK to explore other options such as a fist bump. Ultimately, it is imperative that the child feel like you can comfortably accept their individual need with regard to touch.

Last among the special considerations in work with ASD children with regard to attachment is awareness that unexpected or high levels of emotionality can be difficult for this population. Keeping this in mind, it will often be easiest for ASD youngsters to feel safe and secure with caretakers who are very predictable and low-key in their expression of emotion.

Again, there is probably no group of children in greater need of healing connection than those within the ASD population. These children so need to feel connected and valued by others as a result of having spent so much time feeling *different*. The thoughtful application of the attachment-informed model is exceptionally useful with these children as long as it is done in a manner sensitive to their distinct needs.

This population, as with any child struggling to manage life's challenges, is highly prone to shame concerning their adaptive and relational failures. Increasingly, work with these bright ASD kids has shifted away from ABA to a focus on social cognition and teaching social competence (social cognitive pragmatics) and shame and anxiety management through helping ASD kids better understand their brains as good, just a little different from most brains. This objectifying the child's brain allows for the development of a sense of self as being a little different but not bad; some people are tall, some are short, some have one kind of brain and others a different kind of brain.

The developmental course tends to be far easier for a child or adolescent who experiences their caretaker as understanding their *different brain* not so much as a disability, but rather like all brains with strengths and weaknesses. As these kids experience their caretakers as joyfully celebrating these differences (at least most of them) with PACE, their shame is mitigated and their adaptive path far more likely to go well. This caretaker stance, together with the provision of cognitive tools that help the child use their intellect to navigate social relationships, sets the stage for the ASD child or adolescent's optimal development.

On a number of occasions, I have had the pleasure of sitting with families who have managed to not be lost in fear, worrying about their ASD child's "disability," but rather laughing together concerning some of the adventures that their child's "different brain" had taken them on (e.g. awkward moments with the Transportation Security

Administration, driving the lawn tractor to school). This is in no way to dismiss the challenges faced by these kids or their families, but it is to say that when these challenges are faced with all of the aspects of PACE, relational satisfaction follows.

Reactive attachment disorder and developmental trauma

Children and adolescents presenting with symptoms of reactive attachment disorder (RAD) and severe developmental trauma (DT) are among the most difficult to effectively manage within the treatment milieu. More than any other group, these children are in need of an attachment-informed model of intervention, yet the relentless challenges and wide range of problematic behaviors they present often make this work extremely difficult. These youngsters have a tendency to create chaos around them and to hold tenaciously to a disturbed and disturbing pattern of behavior with limited initial tolerance for positive relational connection or interaction (blocking care).

Often vacillating between intrusive demands, aggression and profound despair, these children greatly challenge anyone faced with the obligation to understand and meet their needs. It is often as if they cannot tolerate the very form of connection essential to their healing. If attachment were a language to be learned, these children grew up through their early stages of life hearing only muffled or chaotic noise, rarely translated or explained by the caregiver into meaningfulness. These children have created their own chaotic relational language and dance that requires the reworking of relational experience from the bottom up.

For these children, the need for caretaker emotional co-regulation in response to their behavior is critical. Children struggling with RAD desperately need all of the attachment-informed insights that have been identified; in fact, much of what has been presented in this text initially came out of research with children with RAD. Having said that, **the consistent provision of these supports to these children is often extremely difficult**.

In the language of Dan Hughes (2007), an expert in RAD and DT, these children often *block their caretaker's care*, which frequently translates into caretakers who out of hopelessness and frustration develop *blocked caring*. In the final analysis, it is the *long game* that we must play with these complicated children; progress will be made little by little as we keep showing up, trying to connect, holding on to our power, remaining hopeful, remaining emotionally regulated and loving, ultimately allowing them to rewrite their relational script to heal. This is slow work!

With this population as much as any, it is imperative that the caretaker maintain their wise and compassionate power. If these children experience the caretaker as undone by their behavior, it creates within them additional anxiety and more problematic behavior. The use of good clinical supervision in work with this population is essential if we are to avoid being pulled off balance and into a mode of providing incoherent and highly reactive responses. As caretakers for these children, it is our responsibility to provide a distinct experience of the relational world, one that is safe and reliable with the goal of moving them towards a secure and safe connection.

Youngsters with RAD and DT can be among the most compelling population with whom we work. As much as they jump up and down on the relational ice to see if they will fall through, those moments in which they reflect an evolving faith in the strength of the ice are truly remarkable and touching. The journey with this population is not for the faint-hearted or those in need of expedient gains. The healing is almost always two steps forward and one back. The critical importance of consistently available relational repair in the wake of a significant emotional or relational tear is as critical as is the caretaker's ability to hold on to their compassionate wisdom and power. These kids require of us that we never let them see us sweat, while at the same time they never experience us as emotionally abandoning.

Psychotic disorders

Even though psychotic disorders, such as schizophrenia, are relatively uncommon in children up through mid to late adolescence, they do exist, and psychotic levels of confusion in children with significant trauma, DT, RAD and ASD are not unusual during heightened stress. This degree of breakdown in one's thought process entails a limited ability to separate what is happening in one's thoughts and feelings from what is occurring in the external environment and is associated with the experience of profound confusion. Auditory hallucinations, phantom-like visual hallucinations, delusions and gross misperceptions are not uncommon in this population of children. In light of this fact, several variants on attachment-informed work with children and adolescents with psychotic symptoms are warranted.

First among these considerations is caution around the use of *playfulness*. Symbolic play (e.g. the stuffed bunny is real), silliness (e.g. pretending to fall down as you get up from the table) and any other form of humor that involves something (playfully) unexpected can be highly confusing, challenging and anxiety producing for these children. The level of confusion and associated apprehension encountered by these young people in their everyday existence often does not allow for much in the way of playfulness.

A second and equally important area of caution with respect to children and adolescents with psychotic thought is their potential apprehension around physical proximity. Much the same as with the ASD population, physical touch can be extremely provocative for these kids and requires thoughtful management of this form of connection. When approaching a situation in which touch might typically be an appropriate form of connection, it is important to seek permission from these children to touch them and comfortably honor their wish should they say "No." Again, as with ASD children, if they indicate that they do not want a hug or shoulder pat, explore other options such as a fist bump and easily accept their stated need whatever it might be.

Once again, similar to the ASD population, in work with these youngsters it is important to have an awareness that unexpected or high levels of emotionality can be difficult. In light of this fact, it will often be easier for youngsters with psychotic features to feel safe and secure with caretakers who are very predictable and relatively low-key in their expression of emotion.

These children often struggle with depression and a profound sense of being alone, yet sadly often find relationships so challenging that they fight to remain isolated. With this fact in mind, it is important to carefully measure our relational efforts with these kids, attempting to carefully read their reactions and tolerances.

An additional factor to keep in mind in work with children with this profile is their propensity for confused and paranoid perceptions concerning the actions and motivations of others. It is important that caretakers working with these youngsters understand this as an aspect of their confusion and not take this perception personally. In the long run, a caretaker's ability to accept (the "A" of the PACE acronym) the distorted perception is critical, avoiding effort to argue for a different perception. There is little value and sometimes high cost in going directly at the child's misperceptions. In time, as the child's sense of safety deepens within an attuned and supportive environment, the profound anxiety that both comes from and further drives psychotic thought reduces and more adaptive and accurate perceptions evolve. The road towards healing for those with a psychotic thought process almost always demands medication intervention and a slow evolution of connection within an environment that is both predictable and safe.

Narcissistically defended children and adolescents

Undoubtedly one of the most difficult dynamics to manage within the treatment milieu is the needs and behaviors of narcissistically defended children or adolescents. This group's compensatory sense of entitlement (compensating for deep feelings of inadequacy), frequent inability to honor authority and powerful, often aggressive, emotional reactivity represent a very real challenge to the clinical caretaker's attachment-informed stance. These difficult but vulnerable children utilize an unconsciously employed (defended) sense of grandiosity to protect them from their true profound underlying feelings of vulnerability. This defended or narcissistic sense of self, although often effective in protecting the individual from conscious awareness of underlying insecurity, does so at significant cost to both relationships and the capacity to learn from experience.

In many respects, self-esteem is organized around two core perceptions: 1. *Am I lovable?*; and 2. *Am I competent?* Those children who have encountered the world as fundamentally affirming both of these self-attributes grow to have sustainable positive or healthy self-esteem. Those who have had too many experiences that have significantly challenged either or both of these variables have self-esteem that is unstable and vulnerable, at times diminished to the point of experiencing the profound anxiety associated with a sense of one's self as unlovable or profoundly incompetent. This anxiety is at a core or primitive level tied to the loss of a fundamental experience of a cohesive and secure self.

A fuller understanding of the narcissistic defense will be approached first by a discussion of healthy or positive self-esteem and then by contrasting this with narcissistic self-esteem.

Healthy self-esteem

Healthy or positive self-esteem allows for the effective, adaptive management of frustration, failure, criticism and rejection and the capacity to learn from these difficult experiences. Central to the functional quality of positive self-esteem is the attribute of flexibility, defined by the capacity to:

- endure injury to one's self-esteem in a limited or circumscribed manner (e.g. failing a math test without succumbing to a profound sense of general incompetence)

- employ self-soothing strategies for self-esteem stabilization and recovery (e.g. following failure on a math test, being able to recall other tests where you have done better and take comfort in the recognition of the relationships in which you are loved and cared for)

- learn from experiences which have challenged one's self-esteem (e.g. in response to failing the math test, accepting the need to study more prior to the next exam).

For individuals with healthy self-esteem, difficult dynamics such as the experience of criticism, rejection or failure result in decreased self-value for a brief period and within a circumscribed aspect of the individual's sense of self. With time and perspective, the individual with positive self-esteem is able to integrate and learn from these experiences, without threat to their fundamental positive sense of who they are (see Figure 12.1).

Example of the character of healthy self-esteem

Ronnie, a 14-year-old, well-liked youngster with good athletic skills, is playing baseball on his middle school team and misses a fly ball hit him to center field. Ronnie knows that he should have caught the ball, but some combination of the angle of the sun and the fact that he had noticed a pretty classmate in the bleachers took him off his game.

Ronnie's initial response was anger at himself and embarrassment, but with a little time, a supportive smile from his mom watching along the third base fence and a playful bit of teasing from his best friend on the bench, he smiles, says, "Sorry, coach," tips the bill of his hat down a bit to block the sun, and decides to speak with Mary in the bleachers after the game and to ignore her for now.

Ronnie was able to take his failed catch, feel the frustration, embarrassment and anger for a moment and then move on to a more regulated state, with a little help from those to whom he was connected. Not only was he able to re-establish a positive emotional state, but he was able to learn from the experience and make accommodations (adjusting his hat, and deciding to put thoughts of Mary off for the moment).

This experience illustrates the flexible and enduring nature of positive self-esteem. Ronnie was able to manage his failure and still be fundamentally OK with himself. The dent in his self-esteem associated with the failed catch did not cause him to plummet into a profound sense of self-disdain, shame, anger and associated anxiety. The flexible nature of his healthy self-esteem allowed it to take a hit, but to have this hit be contained into a sense that he needed to make some changes, not that he was in some way deeply damaged, unlovable or incompetent.

What a gift it is to have this kind of self-esteem, allowing for rejection, criticism or failure to be managed as simply a part of life, not devastating; and, in turn, being able to learn from one's mistakes.

Working within the framework of content presented within this text, we would say that those who have had adequate experiences of *attuned attachment,* affirming their *lovableness,* and the required experiences of *optimal frustration,* allowing a fundamental and evolving sense of competency, will be blessed with positive self-esteem. Those children lacking adequate experience in either or both of these realms are subject to poor or negative self-esteem, demanding a means to manage this difficult sense of self, with employment of a narcissistic defense as one possible response.

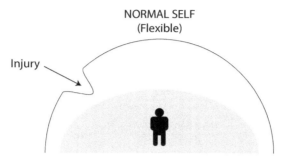

Figure 12.1 Healthy self-esteem

Narcissistic (defended) sense of self

At the core of the narcissistic defense is the unconscious creation of a pseudo-self. This false or defended self protects the individual from awareness of the underlying vulnerable and painfully negative self-assessment of core shame by creating and functioning within a defended and grandiose sense of self. Unfortunately, this defense does not just allow the individual to feel *as good as others*, but rather is characterized by the need to be *better than others*. This overshooting of normative self-esteem not only protects the child or adolescent from profound underlying vulnerability, but also provides a narrative for why they feel so different from others: *they are simply better* (see Figure 12.2).

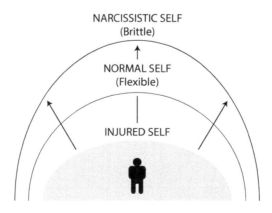

Figure 12.2 Narcissistic defense

Unlike the *flexible* nature of healthy or positive self-esteem, narcissistic self-esteem is characterized by an all-or-nothing quality of *brittleness* (see Figure 12.3). This brittle or glass-like quality results in a pattern in which threats to self-esteem (e.g. criticism, rejection, failure) elicit either no reaction (as if a rock were to bounce off a pane of glass and leave no impact) or a devastating impact (as if shattering the glass).

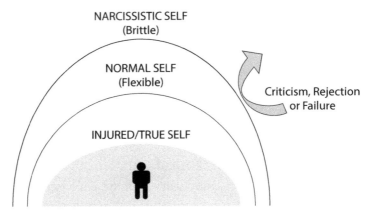

Figure 12.3 Narcissistic injury

In other words, in some instances, the narcissistic child or adolescent will appear indifferent to criticism or failure and show virtually no response, which is generally associated with the attribution of the negative feedback to someone other than themselves (e.g. "I failed the test because it was stupid," "If the coach knew how to coach, I would have done well," "Those kids are idiots that's why they won't let me hang with them"). In other situations, however, they may be highly reactive and express a profound sense of injury and anger, referred to as "narcissistic rage." The emotional intensity of this rage directed at whomever the child experiences as shattering their defense cannot be overstated and is driven by a motivation to retaliate for the profound pain and vulnerability unleashed on the child as a result of the failed narcissistic defense.

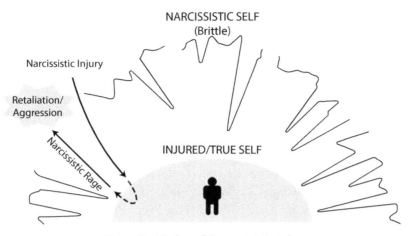

Figure 12.4 Failure of the narcissistic defense

In understanding the power of *narcissistic rage*, it is important to realize the child's response is linked to their momentary exposure to the full thrust of pain and vulnerability accumulated over a lifetime, not simply a reaction to the triggering dynamics or event. Those who have been the object of narcissistic rage from a five- or six-year-old respect it. Those who have been the object of such rage from an older, more sophisticated and powerful individual fear it (see Figure 12.4).

The nature or extent of the narcissistically defended child's or adolescent's response to a threat to self-esteem (e.g. criticism, rejection, failure), although often experienced by others as unpredictable, is generally related to one or more of four interactive triggering dynamics:

1. The child's degree of vulnerability with regard to a particular area of functioning.

   Most narcissistic children or adolescents have areas of functioning in which they are more vulnerable and others in which they are less vulnerable. A narcissistically defended child who has experienced a good deal of academic success is likely to be less reactive to a frustrating learning experience than a child with a learning disability who has experienced a great deal of academic failure. Conversely, a child who has virtually all of their self-esteem linked to a sense of academic competency could be extremely reactive to any perceived threat to this competency. What triggers the failure of the narcissistic defense is often difficult to predict but always goes back to a deep-seated, albeit largely repressed, feeling of inadequacy.

2. The context in which the threat to self-esteem occurs.

    The narcissistic child's or adolescent's experience of threat to self-esteem is significantly increased when it occurs within a public context. The child's reaction to being publicly exposed to others as vulnerable or incompetent is often intolerable, overpowering the defense and releasing the narcissistic rage. For narcissistically defended children, "saving face" is as critical as oxygen; saving face in public even more so. Those working with these children must keep this fact in mind.

3. The cumulative impact of recent or current threats to self-esteem.

    For example, a narcissistic child who plays on a baseball team and generally behaves in an appropriate manner has a game in which he strikes out twice and then misses a catch in the field. After overthrowing the catcher on a play to home, he has a tantrum and walks off the field, throwing his glove and telling the coach that he is an idiot and does not know how to coach. In this case, the series of failures caused the defense to collapse.

4. The nature of the relationship between the child and the individual delivering the injury or challenge to self-esteem.

    Interestingly, this dynamic generally entails an exaggerated response to narcissistic injury when linked to individuals at both ends of the relationship spectrum: those whom the child significantly devalues and those whom he idealizes. In most situations, the narcissistic child is far more likely to exhibit a negative reaction to an individual he perceives as having low status, particularly when that individual is in a position of authority (e.g. hall or bus monitor).

    It is also important to note that these individuals are highly attuned and often reactive to caretakers they experience as emotionally vulnerable, particularly when this vulnerability is expressed in the caretaker's *need* to be respected by the child. Narcissistically defended children and adolescents can sense how troubled caretakers are by their challenges, reading this as weakness, which makes further challenge likely.

In dealing with the exercise of authority from such an individual, the demand to subordinate themselves to a devalued other is a threat to the narcissistic child's self-esteem which is not easily managed. At the other end of the spectrum, however, within a relationship with someone whom he idealizes, the narcissistic child may also be highly reactive. In this situation, the child's value of this individual's approval may be so exaggerated that minor criticism or rejection is experienced as devastating to the defense.

Example of the dysfunctional, brittle quality of the narcissistic defense

Benny, a 13-year-old eighth grader growing up in poverty with an alcoholic single mother, sets off for a day at school. It is early in the morning and his mother was up late drinking the night before and has awakened with a hangover.

(*Italic* represents Benny's thoughts, not his comments.)

Benny: "Bye, mom, I'm going to school."

Mom: "What? Would you stop screaming! Benny, did you clean your room like I told you last night?"

Benny: "I'll do it later. I've got to go."

Mom: "You little bastard. You never do anything I tell you. I swear to God, every day you become more like your father, and if you don't watch it, you'll turn out to be a loser just like that S.O.B!"

Benny: "You old drunk. I don't blame him for leaving you. I don't give a damn what you say."

Benny walks to the bus stop and waits for the bus, which quickly arrives.

Bus driver: "Benny, someone carved in the upholstery back where you were sitting on the bus last night. I think it was you. So I can keep an eye on you, from now on you need to sit up here in the front seat."

Benny: *You stupid old bastard, I didn't do it, but I wish I did. I'll sit up here, not because you told me to, but because the kids at the back of the bus are all jerks and I can't stand to listen to them talk about their pathetic, moronic lives!* [Experience bounces off his brittle narcissistic defense.]

Benny sits where directed by the driver.

Benny arrives at school, walks into his homeroom and is greeted by his teacher, with whom he has a good relationship. His teacher notices that Benny is wearing a new baseball cap and the following exchange occurs:

Teacher: "Good morning, Benny. How are you doing today?"

Benny: "Okay."

Teacher: "Hey, is that a new Cubs hat?"

Benny: "Yeah."

Teacher: "I like it. I respect that you are a loyal fan. Even though the poor Cubs can't win a game to save themselves, you stand behind them."

Benny: "I don't care about the Cubs, I just like the hat."

Teacher: "OK, but I tell you the Cubs could use some brave loyal supporters. Hey, remember the new rule on hats and be sure to take it off when the bell rings, OK?"

Benny: *My hair looks like hell ever since my mom tried to cut it. I am not taking this hat off and having other kids give me crap about my hair.*

Teacher: "Benny, did you hear me about the hat? Look, it's not my rule but I do have to enforce it. So please take it off and stick it in your pocket."

Benny: [Ignoring the teacher and sitting quietly at his desk.] *I am not taking this hat off. I take enough crap from everyone and I am just not doing it.*

Teacher: [Walking back to Benny's desk, attempting not to draw much attention to himself or the exchange with Benny.] "Benny, you really do have to take your hat off. I'm sorry, but it's the rule."

The teacher then gently reaches over and removes Benny's hat by the bill. [**CRASH! The defense shatters.**]

> Benny: [Grabs a chair and raises it over his head.] "Give me back my hat, you S.O.B., or I swear I'll kill you!"

In this scenario, the origin of Benny's violent rage is not the injury associated with his well-meaning teacher's request that he remove his hat. Rather, this incident illustrates a common dynamic in which aggressive behavior is associated with the failure of the narcissistic defense in the face of a combination or serial impact of minor injuries to the child's self-esteem (i.e. the comments from his mother and the bus driver, together with the prospect of public humiliation concerning his hair). With his teacher's removal of his hat, Benny became flooded by profoundly painful, underlying insecurities, triggering a retaliation for the full sum of this pain against a teacher who inadvertently pushed his brittle defense beyond its breaking point.

Unfortunately, a heavy reliance upon a narcissistic defense for the management of underlying insecurity not only explodes in episodes of narcissistic rage, but also entails a number of less dramatic but equally difficult dynamics.

First among these is, as noted earlier, the fact that the brittle nature of this defended sense of self results in a limited ability to tolerate and learn from criticism or failure, since negative feedback is generally disregarded or deflected. If one's profound need to preserve an inflated sense of self results in a psychological process that shields awareness of more subtle failures and automatically projects blame for such failures upon others, the critical process of trial-and-error learning is dramatically undermined.

Second, the social ramifications of this defense are highly significant and extremely complicated, particularly in light of the fact that one of the primary dynamics promoting the need for the defense relates to insecurity concerning the quality of one's relationships and the ability to elicit caring responses from others. Socially, the individual who relies heavily upon a narcissistic defense needs and demands from others a great deal of affirmation of their grandiosity. In many respects, they value relationships with others only when these serve to reflect back their inflated sense of self, resulting in an interpersonal style that reflects entitlement and is limited in compassionate attunement to the needs of others. This style of relating, unless performed with tremendous sophistication and skill (as in narcissistic charismatic leaders), draws or elicits considerable resentment and criticism from others, thus further supporting the individual's underlying sense that others will not find them worthy of respect or love.

Attuned, attachment-informed support of the narcissistic child or adolescent

Central to effective work with narcissistically defended kids is awareness that no one chooses this path of development; rather, they are cast onto it as result of highly painful and debilitating early life experiences. These youngsters are not easy to manage in that they are often threatened by seemingly benign interactions, particularly with persons in authority. In work with these kids, it is essential to remember that it is an underlying or core sense of shame that drives the defense, which demands of the empathically attuned caretaker moment-to-moment insight on how to avoid any more activation of this intolerable shame than is absolutely necessary.

Core to effective work with the narcissistic child is the balance between the caretaker's use of authority and compassionate understanding of the child's underlying vulnerability. The child's grandiosity should be challenged gently in a manner that does not precipitate the complete failure of the narcissistic defense. Effective intervention demands a careful attunement to the child's range of *optimal frustration* with respect to challenges to self-esteem, while remembering that to the narcissistic child, preservation of this defense is as essential as oxygen.

In many respects, the use of narcissism as a psychological defense is analogous to the biological process involved in the body's development of a fever to thwart infection. As with a fever, this adaptive response solves one problem while creating others. In responding to narcissism, we must remain focused on both primary and secondary dynamics; in the analogy, the cause of the fever and the management of the fever.

Understanding narcissism dictates an intervention process that addresses both the underlying negative self-beliefs (infection) and the narcissistic attitudes and sense of entitlement (fever). To this end, the following intervention insights and guidelines are offered:

- A narcissistic defense is never taken away from a child. The child will give it up when they no longer need it.

- The child will no longer need their narcissistic defense when their underlying negative self-assessments are replaced by improved feelings of being loved and competence.

- The goal in management of the narcissistic child's behavior is to bend, but not break, their defense and to recognize an approximation of appropriate response as a step towards healthier functioning (optimal frustration).

These few statements provide the framework for understanding and guiding intervention with narcissistic children and adolescents. As stated above, effective work with these children and adolescents demands a delicate balance in which their sense of entitlement is challenged, but not in such a powerful manner that their defenses fail completely. Unfortunately, conceptualizing this balance is far easier than actually achieving it.

Work with these youngsters is often profoundly frustrating. To be in the presence of a child who has an extremely limited ability to honor our basic right to be treated as an equal, let alone to defer to our authority as adults, is for most of us an unpleasant experience. These children often overtly disregard the needs and wants of others, and in doing so elicit indignation. Management of our own frustration and natural desire to retaliate against the narcissistic child's sense of entitlement and inability to defer to authority is truly one of the most difficult aspects of work with this population.

Ultimately, effective work with these children is predicated upon our ability to manage the inherent assault on our own self-esteem produced by a child whose defense may well require the negation of our own worth. The profound struggle for supremacy playing out between two individuals with narcissistic vulnerabilities is not a foreign occurrence within the treatment setting. As a matter of fact, one of the most frequent dynamics in which profoundly aggressive behavior erupts from the narcissistic child or adolescent involves a difficult interaction with a narcissistically vulnerable clinical caretaker.

Adults with significant narcissistic vulnerabilities themselves may voice such folksy attitudes as: "That kid needs to be brought down a notch!" or, "That kid has a chip on his shoulder that I plan to knock off for him!" We must recognize that if an intervention program for this population is to be effective, we must identify staff who have an effective interpersonal style for work with these children. It has been my experience that in the absence of attention to this variable, regardless of the quality of a program's other factors, effective intervention will not occur.

The process of challenging, without destroying, a narcissistic child's defense demands tremendous attunement to the child's inner state, as well as a patient, long-term perspective. We must remember that real change for these children occurs over time, not as a result of winning an individual battle or power struggle; however, effective intervention is equally predicated upon the adult's absolute clarity concerning both the child's need for the adult to be in charge and the adult's capacity to compassionately do so. The issue of power is an ever-present focus in the world of the narcissistic child or adolescent, particularly with respect to their sense of power relative to others.

Effective work with these children requires that the caretaker have both an innate sense of their own personal power and vulnerabilities and clear empathic attunement to the child's need to preserve self-esteem. The narcissistic child's perception of the caretaker as powerful reduces the challenge associated with subordination to the caretaker. When the narcissistic child subordinates himself to someone perceived as having great power, he experiences a more limited threat to his own grandiosity; however, subordination to someone perceived as weak or incompetent is a significant threat to his self-esteem.

The caretaker who is perceived as both powerful and compassionate lowers the child's general level of anxiety and increases the potential for healing challenges to the defense that fall within the range of optimal frustration. It is important to recognize that the definition of power is not that of physical or intellectual power, but rather compassionate wisdom and security; a caretaker whom the child recognizes as un-threatened by them, in no manner *needing* the child to affirm them. This caretaker is caring and supportive, yet reflects confidence and competence in the process of managing the child.

Achieving a compassionate and balanced use of power with the narcissistic child is not a simple task. To this end, the following guidelines are offered:

- Honor approximations of subordination. Do not demand that the child comply exactly as directed, allow for some degree of resistance, and do not require that the child carry out his compliance with a pleasant attitude.

- Avoid bringing your own charged emotion to confrontational interactions. Stay calm.

- Exhibit patience and avoid moving too quickly to threatening consequences for non-compliance. Do not expect or demand immediate or complete compliance. Give the child time to comply and let them use their slow pace to save face.

- Do not lecture or moralize. Simply state your directive clearly and, when necessary, outline the logical consequence for non-compliance. Say what you need to say but then keep quiet.

- Do not express a desperate need for the child to comply. Again, stay calm. If the child senses in the adult a desperate need for them to comply, the weakened position associated with this need may well elicit resistance. **WATCH your non-verbal cues: They need to express respect for the child, recognition of the poignancy of the moment and kindness.**

- After a difficult encounter, find a private opportunity to acknowledge your sense of remorse (make the repair) that the problem occurred and, if appropriate, your appreciation that the child ultimately complied with your directive.

- Attempt to identify together a plan that would avoid a recurrence of this situation.

Example of the effective employment of these principles

Sam, a difficult, narcissistically defended 15-year-old patient, has come into group in an upbeat mood, laughing and talking with a friend. The therapist indicates it is time for the group to begin; however, Sam's exuberant mood persists and he continues to talk to his friend. In the first moments of group, Sam receives two gentle requests from the therapist to quiet down. After about two minutes of continued talking and laughter, however, the therapist warns Sam that if he continues to make it difficult, he will be asked to leave the group and that she would really miss him if she had to ask him to do so.

Approximately six minutes into the group, Sam is still being silly and disruptive. At this point the therapist makes another attempt to connect and direct, playfully stating, "Sam, not that I don't love to see you happy, but you aren't quieting down and it is making it hard for me to run the group. As much as I enjoy your good company, this has to be my last warning—if you are having just too much fun to quiet down, I am going to ask you to leave for today. You're not in trouble—it just isn't working today."

For the moment Sam sits quietly, appearing to contemplate his options, and then begins to laugh out loud, saying how boring the group is. The therapist ignores this comment and returns to the group topic, ignoring Sam for approximately the next 30 seconds, and then as Sam continues to talk out loud, she quietly, but clearly, states, "Sam, I've got to ask you to leave. You are welcome back tomorrow, but I want you to leave for the rest of the hour."

The therapist returns to the group for approximately a minute, then turns to Sam and says, "Sam, I don't want to struggle about this, but I have asked you to leave." The therapist then sits quietly, ceasing to run the group while waiting for Sam to leave.

Sam then asks, "What are you waiting for?" The therapist does not respond and ultimately, Sam asks, "What are you going to do if I don't leave?"

The therapist calmly responds, "I'm not certain, Sam. I hope that you'll do what I am asking, because if you don't, I won't be able to run group."

At this point several of the other group members indicate to Sam that he should go. Sam angrily stands and proclaims, "This group is bullshit and you are an asshole. No problem, I'm out of here!" Sam knocks his chair around as he gets up to leave and he walks out the door with the parting offering, "See you later, chumps. I need a nap and Dr. Asshole wants me to go take one."

Once Sam has left the group, the therapist calmly states to the rest of the class, "I'm sorry this had to play out this way, I enjoy having Sam as part of our group and hope we can work things out so he can come back and remain with us." Then she returns to the group process with no further comment concerning Sam or the incident.

Up to this point the therapist has handled this situation with skill and grace. She has remained calm, avoided threats, refused to argue, given Sam time to respond, and avoided backing him into a corner as much as possible—always trying to remain connected with him; however, effective work with Sam now requires that his therapist attempt a *relational repair* with him prior to their next group. This takes the form of an interaction similar to the one that follows:

Later in the day, the group therapist finds a means to speak with Sam alone in the hallway. She opens her exchange with the statement, "I'm sorry group didn't go well for us today."

Sam, still angry, responds, "It would have gone fine if you had just relaxed and not been into your power thing."

To this, his therapist responds, "Sam, I know it seems to you that I was unreasonable. I'm sorry that you can't understand the way the situation felt to me, but I did what I thought I needed to do. But that's not really what I wanted to talk to you about. I have two things to say. First, I know that the situation in group was hard for you today, and I appreciate that you did leave when I asked you to, and second, I want to see if we can find some way to avoid putting each other in that situation again. I really want you in the group, you are so smart and have so much to offer. Do you have any ideas?"

At this point, kids are often unable to offer much in the way of a constructive suggestion and will generally express either indifference or rejection of the idea of a plan. The adult will need to tolerate the child's apparent indifference to their effort. The responsibility to generate a plan that would be useful to both the therapist and child will in most situations fall almost exclusively upon the adult, who at the same time must state that it is not a plan unless they both agree upon it. In Sam's case, it will not be a good idea for him to re-enter the group until there is some form of agreement. This could be as loose as, "We will give it one more effort without a plan and then if it doesn't go well, we will have to do something different."

Conclusion on narcissistically defended children and adolescents

Effective work with narcissistically defended children can be highly challenging. These children demand of their caregivers tremendous patience, self-restraint and capacity for forgiveness, couched within a clear sense of security and comfort in their capacity for the wise and compassionate expression of authority. This constellation of needs is often far easier to meet when supporting a younger child than when approaching a more powerful, sophisticated and potentially dangerous adolescent. Nonetheless, the needs of both the younger and older child struggling with a narcissistic adaptation are quite similar. The importance of remembering their profound fear of humiliation and underlying vulnerability is central to their effective and compassionate management.

> *Note:* It is helpful to remember that the **only** way in which the need for this defense will be resolved is through the healing of the underlying profoundly negative perception and experiences of self. This healing requires a great deal of PACE and repaired tears. **Again, the narcissistic defense can never be taken from the child; rather, they will be able to give it up when it is no longer needed.** This healing will come through their experience of connection and optimal frustration, allowing for an evolving, cohesive and coherent sense of self as lovable and competent.

Chapter 13

SPECIAL STRATEGIES AND CONSIDERATIONS FOR MILIEU-BASED ATTACHMENT-FOCUSED TREATMENT

Touch, Food, Unexpected Positive Reactions, Transitional Objects and Peer-Centric Milieus

Touch

Sadly, nurturing touch has been the object of much misguided consideration and regulation within our child and adolescent treatment programs. Being a central avenue for connection and nurturance, touch must be a part of any treatment program for children and adolescents struggling with issues of trauma and attachment. Clearly, touch must be managed in a clinically informed manner guided by both the individual child's needs and the comfort and connective style of the caretaker.

In understanding non-verbal communication as the *language of the heart*, the healing of children with *broken hearts* requires mindful and compassionate use of all avenues of each communication. Whether working with a young child or an adolescent, provided the child is able to tolerate it, the use of gentle and playful touch is a strong connecting force. If a treatment setting has an injunction against appropriate touch between caretakers and child or child to child, it is at the cost of accessing one of the most healing aspects of human behavior.

In holding this position, it is in no way meant to suggest that all touch is good or healing, for the needs of each individual and the nature of the touch must be taken into consideration. Complicating the discernment of the appropriateness of touch is the potential for touch to have a sexualized dynamic. The presence of this dynamic is determined unilaterally by a sense of crossing of a sexual boundary by either person. When a sexual boundary violation is sensed by either a staff member or child, it must be brought to light and discussed in the context of clinical supervision and therapy. These moments are not destructive or clinically contra-indicated as long as they are managed with openness. Staff who are frequently experienced as uncomfortable by children or adolescents require more intensive clinical supervision or movement to a different position. Conversely, staff who are not able to comfortably approach appropriate touch due to personal style or fear of allegations of inappropriate touch also require more intensive clinical supervision or placement in a setting not requiring this capacity.

Touch is such an important aspect of connection within the attachment-informed milieu model that it must remain a regular focus of discussion within staff orientation as well as group and individual supervision, for it is as complicated as it is critical.

Food

Within relational dynamics and attachment, food serves as a powerful and primitive reflection of caring and a potent reinforcement and pathway to social engagement. In light of how central food is to our survival and how it was the focus and function of our primitive tribal cultures, to not consider how food is approached within the treatment setting is an important opportunity lost; and in some situations, its mismanagement can be a profound detriment to the relational healing that lies at the core of our treatment goals.

It is beyond the scope of this work to explore the issue of food within the family and/or treatment setting, yet how it is managed in the caretaking relationship is so important that it demands some mention in the discussion of attachment-informed milieu-based work. The act of being fed and protected are the two principle early life functions of the caretaker–child relationship. It is through the mother's attunement to the child and the child learning that their crying draws their mother to attend to their hunger that much of the reciprocal dance of attachment unfolds. It is in both the offering and receiving of nurturance that connection evolves. This being the case, we are obligated in our work with children who come to us with complicated relational histories to carefully consider the role and power of food in the healing process. To this end, food in the treatment setting will be discussed as important with regard to being fed, feeding others and food in the context of community.

Being fed

There are few experiences more universally positive than that of being offered something inviting to eat. Our bodies are wired from our sense of smell to our response to the visual experience of food, to seek and value it as sustaining to our lives. This experience of food, except when overridden by other factors such as in the case of anorexia or physical illness, draws us towards connection with those offering sustenance.

Should food be offered to a child in a manner suggesting caretaker ambivalence, indifference or resentment, the resulting anxiety for the child is nearly inevitable, as his survival is dependent upon the caretaker's ability and desire to feed him. Within the treatment setting, the responsibility for feeding the child belongs to the setting and those within it in this role. When this is done with little attention to the quality and nature of the feeding experience, much opportunity is lost and perhaps unintended harm incurred.

Ideas for enhancing the nurturing and connecting role of food in the treatment setting

- Invite the program's food preparation staff to be a part of the community. Encourage them to (joyfully) serve the food and to check in with the kids at each meal to see how it was. Have the cooks regularly discuss with the kids what they do and do not like about the food and meals. Help the kids see the people who are preparing their food as truly caring for them, fulfilling their role with loving care.

- Make sure the food is appetizing and is presented in an attractive manner.

- Make the environment where food is served pleasant and with some degree of social engagement—do not let a child sit alone when eating.

- Have food available that is a special liking of each child, and help staff know and acknowledge what the child likes and does not like—this is an important aspect of the child's feeling known, reflecting your knowledge that you know they really like this food.

- Be thoughtful about using food as a reinforcement. This is very complicated in that withholding of the reinforcement is implied when the child is out of compliance. We do not want to inadvertently use withholding food as a punishment. Would we withhold oxygen, water or protection from predators? I don't think so, yet food (symbolically) is just as essential.

- Have healthy food available for eating when children are hungry. For children with weight issues, these are managed by the nature of the food available.

Feeding others

In our recognition of the attachment-linked importance of a *sense of purpose*, supporting children and adolescents in having the opportunity to prepare food for the community can be very helpful. There are few human interactions more powerful than that of giving and receiving nourishment; within the treatment setting, we do not want to miss the opportunity for the children and adolescents to have the connecting and healing experience of preparing and serving food to others.

Ideas to support the joy of feeding others

- Have each child rotate in to help kitchen staff in food preparation. This must be done in a manner that allows the child to feel like an important part of the food preparation and serving.

- Have teams of children work together on a regular basis to plan and prepare food for the community.

- Have individuals or teams prepare snacks or dessert for the community.

- Make a cookbook of favorite recipes made by children.

- Invite families in for special events with meals prepared by the children.

- Have family meetings following a meal prepared by the child.

Eating in community

Mealtime within the family, tribe or treatment community is one of our most open moments for social engagement. This being the case, it is important to mark and use this time as effectively as possible. The use of *ritual* as a means of setting time apart as "a special moment" enhances this moment's psychological importance. This can be done in many ways, but must be managed by caretakers as if the ritual is important or it will carry little weight as part of social enculturation and connection.

Examples of meal-related rituals

» Prior to anyone eating, all must be served and the cook must be thanked for the offering.

» Each individual at the meal will note one thing for which they are grateful prior to eating.

» At the end of the meal, each individual thanks the people who prepared the food.

» No one leaves the meal until all have finished.

» At the end of the meal, the staff review the next events in the day prior to leaving mealtime.

» At the beginning of each meal, prior to eating, people are given the opportunity to make announcements or ask the community for help with an issue.

» A *values-clarification prompt* is provided at the beginning of each meal as a topic for possible discussion. This would not be the only topic allowed—just support for conversation (e.g. "Which is more important: telling the truth or kindness?").

» A minute's (guided or unguided) mindfulness activity prior to beginning to eat.

Our culture has become increasingly secular, which means that religious rituals (e.g. prayer before a meal) are much less frequently practiced within most families. It is important to note that shared rituals are part of the process of defining one's sense of belonging to others and that rituals that have historically been religious can be replaced with secular rituals that have much the same impact on one's sense of belonging (e.g. fraternal organization rituals, rituals associated with patriotism).

It should also be noted that the practice of mealtime rituals may be relatively uncomfortable for those who have not practiced rituals as an important part of their lives. In light of this, and the fact and the reality that the ritual will only carry the connecting and healing importance that the supporting staff give it, it is critical that staff supervising meal rituals be able to convey to the community their importance. This may require a good deal of modeling on the part of staff who are more practiced in the use of ritual, for staff who are less so. **Rituals only have the magic we are able to convey they have.**

Unexpected positive reactions

A counterintuitive interactional strategy that can be helpful in treatment settings serving children and adolescents with highly provocative and challenging behaviors is the clinical caretaker's presenting a positive and appreciative response to some of these behaviors. In this response, the caretaker frames positively, in both their words and affect, a sense that what the child has done was in some important manner helpful. Baylin and Hughes (2016) discuss this intervention eloquently in their text *The Neurobiology of Attachment-Focused Therapy*, providing a brain-based understanding for why a *positive highly unexpected caretaker response* to challenging behavior can be so healing in positively rewiring the brain.

Example of presenting a positive response
to challenging behavior

Maria is a provocative and challenging ten-year-old girl, with whom I have worked for several years.

One day, after Maria and I had finished our regular weekly session in my office, as was our ritual we were heading outside for the last ten minutes of our time to pass a small football. Happily and cooperatively walking down the office drive to a place where we could pass the ball, we passed by a clear plastic basement window well covering. Before I noticed, Maria took two steps towards the window enclosure and stomped on it, shattering the plastic into pieces, immediately freezing and looking up to me for my reaction. Having just read Baylin and Hughes's (2016) book and wanting desperately to not replicate the response that Maria generally gets for such actions, I offered the following: "Oh my goodness! Maria I had no idea that enclosing was so fragile and dangerous. I so appreciate you showing me this to help protect anyone from getting hurt. Boy, I did not know that thing could break like that, but now I do, thanks to you"— which I managed to carry off as an expression of genuine appreciation.

In response, Maria stood silent for five to ten seconds (which never happens), staring at me with a somewhat frozen look of confusion as I thanked her for her help, her response reflecting what I now believe to be a sign of her brain rewiring. In my more typical response, I would have offered a well-modulated, "Maria, I know that things like that window just call out to us sometimes to be whacked, but please try not to do this because I now must replace the window." This would have likely gone fine without increased escalation, but at the same time not much therapeutic benefit.

As I think about the rewiring of the brain in response to single or limited experiences, I realize that I have bought into this idea completely with respect to traumatic events, never having considered the potential for a positive event to similarly rewrite neural pathways; however, if this is the case, as the neurosciences seem to be showing us, what wonderful doors it might open for work within our treatment settings. I do not believe that all such difficult behavior can or should be managed in this manner but, when it is possible, there is little to be lost and perhaps much to be gained in this response. This noted, it is also important to keep in mind that this means of responding requires of the caretaker the ability to very effectively express positive affect in their response. Should this not be the case, the child or adolescent is likely to experience the caretaker's response as sarcastic and/or manipulative, neither of which will promote in the child positive change.

This is not easy! In the case of Maria and the broken window, I was faced with a need to suppress a very real sense of, "Oh God, I now have to fix that damn thing!"; however, the clarity of the Baylin and Hughes (2016) presentation on this topic allowed me to place the window repair as secondary to the opportunity to help this sweet, complicated kid heal.

Further examples of positive responses to challenging behavior

> » "I was going to eat the cookie you just threw on the floor, but do you know what? I really am getting kind of fat and need to stop eating stuff like that—I guess I kind of need to thank you for helping me with this—I have so little willpower around food."

> » "You know the way you snuck out of the room during group really helped me see how dangerous it is when we have the little kids in this room—one of those guys could slip out and really be in trouble. Thanks, Billy, I will let the younger classroom know of this issue with their kids."

> » "You know, when you called me an 'asshole' it kind of got my attention, and I began to realize that I probably wasn't treating you guys as fairly as I want to."

> » "When you slammed that doors on me, I realized how large and dangerous those doors could be and that we should probably see if we can get them replaced—I had never noticed this before. I guess I have you to thank for helping me realize that those things need to be fixed—somebody could really get hurt."

Again, for those interested in learning more about the neuroscience of attachment and the brain science behind this strategy, please read

Baylin and Hughes's excellent book, *The Neurobiology of Attachment-Focused Therapy* (2016).

Transitional objects

D.W. Winnicott's (1958) concept of "transitional objects," later slightly reinterpreted by Daniel Stern (1985) as a "personified object," refers to objects used in a ritualistic manner by individuals to support themselves in invoking the soothing emotional memory of a comforting other. Common examples of these include a child's security blanket, stuffed animal, their own thumb, or in adults such things as a wedding ring, picture of family or keepsake passed down from a parent. These objects gain their power to support emotional regulation through their simple invoking of a sense of the trusted caretaker, and/or through the caretaker–child positive intersubjective experience of the object as having the *magic* to calm and soothe.

In short, objects that can be used to support children and adolescents in feeling less alone and safer are important tools to be used within the intensive treatment setting. It is beyond the scope of this offering to discuss in detail all of the ways *transitional objects* serve to support development. Nonetheless, a treatment community that honors their role can be seen as gaining the following:

- A tool to help soothe a child when they are blocking care from caretakers.

- An object that can be soothing and available when other supports are less available (e.g. during the night, when on a therapeutic trial visit, in the *quiet room*, post discharge).

- A means for "playful" intersubjectivity between the caretaker and child (e.g. as they join in play affirming that bunny is very real).

- A child's reliance on a stuffed animal helps staff remember how truly little and vulnerable they are, even when they seem so powerful in their ability to challenge.

- When staff have and share their own playful (regressed) relationship with a stuffed animal, it reduces the child's shame in needing comfort in anything that can offer it.

Ways in which transitional objects can be used in the treatment milieu:

- At admission, children may use their own stuffed animal or choose one from the options available. The animal becomes the child's possession. Children who do not wish to choose an animal will work with their clinician to think about what animal they might ultimately like. If after a set period a child will not choose an animal, the clinician will make a choice of one for the child; the animal will stay in the clinician's office until the child wants the animal or is discharged with it.

- For adolescents, boys in particular, the regressive nature of the use of a stuffed animal as a transitional object may be embarrassing in a manner that makes them impossible to use. For these kids, things such as a photo of a family pet, or a favorite breed of dog, or a small rock that the therapist has carried with them for a week, and so on, can be used as a transitional object.

- Staff can have their own stuffed animal as well, and the various animals may have relational life with one another. (All are "real," in the language of the Velveteen Rabbit.)

- If a child destroys or loses an animal, this is managed in a very important and sensitive manner.

- It is important to recognize that therapeutic pets often serve the same role as a transitional object and can be used in the same manner.

Many of the children served within our intensive treatment settings have had such limited or problematic attachment histories that they have very little in the way of experience of safety within relationships. For these children, the use of transitional objects is complicated, yet sometimes one of the initial building blocks of relational capacity. For these kids, the use of the stuffed animal is more one of "self-projection" than a bridge to a relationship with another. This does not mean that special stuffed animals are not useful for these kids, but rather that we are likely to see projected onto the animal the child's feelings about themselves—sometimes lovable and perhaps sometimes absolutely not. In the child's movement towards more consistently being able to care for and love their animal, they become better able to risk allowing others into connection with them. As noted above, management of a child's indifference or destructive rage towards their animal must be handled in a gentle and thoughtful manner; as always, leading us back to PACE.

When a treatment milieu can embrace a child's or adolescent's core need to feel lovable and not alone, through whatever means is accessible, we most open the door to healing.

Peer-centric milieus

The vast majority of our intensive child and adolescent treatment milieus operate within an adult-centric model, wherein staff play the central role in developing, instilling and enforcing the culture; a model that places virtually all power and authority in the hands of the supervising adults. In work with younger children, there are relatively few options but to adopt such a model, in that children of this age often have very limited capacity to objectively observe themselves and/or make a stable commitment to the best interest of a peer group or peer culture. This being the case, the discussion of peer-centric clinical milieus is more typically appropriate in consideration of work with adolescent populations.

At the core of the child-centric milieu is a clinical and administrative culture that attempts to empower the community of peers to form and enforce cultural values and norms. In work with adolescents, this model more closely emulates the outside culture and supports gains made within the clinical setting to be more easily transferred to the post-treatment setting. Having adolescents play a prosocial leadership role additionally supports attachment development through the establishment of a sense of purpose, the third stage of attachment development discussed earlier.

Adolescents from backgrounds of poor or limited relational attunement come into treatment, not only with the typical adolescent issues around authority and associated normative drive for autonomy, but also, due to these problematic early caretaker relationships, a heightened struggle in the capacity to trust in the care of any adult. For these young people, the peer group often represents a new and evolving opportunity for connection and safety in community. For both the typical and relationally challenged adolescent, this opening sets the stage for banding together in the creation of their own culture and/or push back against the adult culture. If this natural process of seeking community in the culture of peers can be prosocially harnessed in the treatment setting, it both serves to minimize the frequency of the emotionally triggering adult–adolescent power struggles and provides a context for healing the child's approach to relationships with greater potential for carryover post discharge.

The power and utility of a peer-centric clinical milieu noted, the process of establishing such a program represents a delicate balancing act on the part of the clinical staff if they are to be helpful in shaping the culture, but not so controlling that it becomes theirs (adult-centric). This process requires of the staff a tolerance for the organic process of group culture formation, periodic expression of peer values inconsistent with adult values, and the ability to hang back and let the peer culture operate. This is in no way meant to suggest that staff do not ultimately have responsibility to assure safety and prosocial dynamics within the milieu, but it is to say that for the culture to be peer-centric, staff supervisors must give a relatively wide berth to the culture's process. The initial step in this process is to create an administrative or governance framework.

Creating a peer-centric milieu structure

In implementing a peer-centric milieu, it is generally best to utilize an existing governing structure such as the US constitution as a model for clinical milieu management. This structure can be modified, but should remain more or less consistent with the intent of the components of governance associated with the model.

Example of peer-centric milieu modeled upon the US constitution

This strategy of milieu management demands that the clinical administrative supervisors write a constitution for eventual ratification by the adolescent population. The constitution must be written in a way that truly empowers the peer group but always places the final responsibility for milieu safety and compassionate care on the staff. The staff write the constitution but it is to be amended and ratified by the peer community on the unit at its inception. Following this initial implementation, the peer community may amend the constitution with a super majority of the peers in agreement and with approval by staff.

Sample treatment program peer-centric constitution

Basic beliefs and rights:

- All peers are created equal and come with and maintain within the milieu certain rights and responsibilities.

Constitutionally guaranteed rights:

- To be treated with respect and kindness by peers and staff.

- To be free from overly coercive behavioral control by peers or staff.

- To speak one's truth, attempting to do so in a manner that is respectful to others and promotes being understood.

- To take space when struggling with emotions, with the understanding that when kids are struggling, a peer or staff member will remain close by to provide support as needed.

- To be included in discussions concerning one's own treatment and discharge.

- To select and use a peer advocate in any meeting for which the child's parents approve their participation.

Constitutionally supported responsibilities:

- To attend milieu-based meetings whenever possible.

- To provide clear and compassionate feedback and counsel to others.

- To help maintain safety within the milieu.

- To make the milieu an inviting setting free of intimidation and unkindness.

Branches of peer-centric government
Executive branch
Peer council: Three children selected by peers; must have full unit privileges while on council. Council meets daily with staff to discuss the milieu and the needs of individual peers. Executive branch will make decisions on milieu management to be approved by staff, based upon their accordance with the *rights and responsibilities* outlined in the constitution.

Judicial branch
Peer review group: Three children selected by peers to serve in review of peer infractions and recommend corrective actions. Staff or peer council may refer an individual or situation for peer review.

Legislative branch
Community council: Made up of all children with daily meetings to discuss any aspects of milieu life. Staff serve as counsel to this group but do not run the meetings. Any issue for which there is majority agreement will be sent to the executive branch for consideration.

Peer advocate: The person playing this role is mutually agreed upon by the child, the advocate and the staff. This person may attend any meetings as an advocate for the child, provided staff and guardians approve their presence (family meetings with a peer advocate can be remarkably useful).

The offering above is a very simple illustration of a means by which to structure a peer-centric milieu; much additional thought and management must go into the actual implementation within any clinical setting. There are many special situations and dynamics that must be considered for this model to be effective and safe. Issues such as length of stay, child cognitive profile and staff temperament, to mention a few, demand thoughtful tailoring of this model to any setting. This noted, it remains my belief that the culture of the peer group is often under-utilized within treatment settings and that when thoughtfully empowered, this culture has a *magic* that the adult world does not.

In using the peer culture to help in the healing of one another, the peers are given the gift of purpose and a framework for a resource that can be utilized after discharge.

It is important to remember in the use of this model that it is critical that the staff supervisors attempt to stand back whenever possible and let the power of the peer culture work; for if staff become overactive, they run the risk of the community becoming cynical concerning their own power and/or authority and the result is a milieu without a center.

Chapter 14

THE ROLE OF KINDNESS IN TREATMENT

kind·ness
/ˈkīn(d)nəs/
noun: **kindness**
The quality of being friendly, generous and considerate.

It may seem peculiar to take a strong stand on the critical importance of *kindness* to effective work within child and adolescent treatment programs any more than it would seem necessary to recommend feeding these children regularly. The often challenging and disempowering nature of the attitudes, beliefs and behavior of the children within these programs, however, too often draws clinical caretakers towards negative and/or harsh styles of interaction that are in fact "unkind." Kindness is not defined as giving the child what they want, or always being able to respond with a sweet and accepting tone, **but it is never forgetting that at their core these kids are sad, confused, frightened, angry, lonely, ashamed, hopeless and lost, and that they are doing the best they can in the context of this reality**. Remembering this allows us a stance in which we **always** do our best to express compassion regardless of what the child's troubled inner world visits upon us. In Chapter 8, the discussion of holding on to one's power in limit setting examines in more detail the imperative of compassionate management of difficult behavior.

There is no variable more powerful to the development of a sense of safe and secure connection between a caretaker and a child than the simple consistent expression of kindness. Such expression is predicated on empathy and compassion, even if, or perhaps particularly if, a child is struggling with us. Kindness is expressed primarily through the soft non-verbals such as a shared smile, frown, tear or a gentle gesture of touch.

With the population of children and adolescents served within milieu-based programs, overt expression of kindness may initially elicit a somewhat anxious or distancing response. This can be understood in many ways; nonetheless, the healing power of kindness in rewriting a child's experience and narrative concerning relationships is ultimately undeniable, making efforts at responding to these kids in a neutral or harsh manner counter-therapeutic and unacceptable within the treatment setting.

Kindness demands of the clinical caretaker the ability to readily repair torn relationships, to forgive quickly, and often the profound gentleness associated with catching a floating soap bubble without causing it to break. It is often not intuitive or easy to return kindness to a threat, a challenge or even an assault, yet this is what is required if we are to be a healing force in these children's lives, helping them rewrite their own stories as well as their stories about others.

In short, it is the act of kindness that conveys the compassion that, together with wisdom, affords us the power to heal the broken inner lives of these unfortunate, complicated yet resilient children who end up in intensive treatment programs.

CONCLUSION

It is my deep belief that attachment-informed work within our intensive treatment settings is our best hope to support healing in the vulnerable and complicated young people they serve. This approach is neither easy nor natural to all clinical caretakers, but it can be taught and implemented when made a priority. When effectively implemented, this model provides a coherent pathway to healing for the children and adolescents it serves, as well as a sense of purpose and well-being for those serving in the role of clinical caretakers.

At the heart of this work is our capacity to allow children the powerful and important experience of "feeling felt" (intersubjectivity). In the deep sense of connection associated with this experience lies the road to learning to regulate emotions, develop a positive self-narrative and learn to live in community. No other developmental need impacts a child across as many domains of adaptive functioning as does the experience of connection and attachment. When the child is held within a safely connected relationship, the challenges of growing up are manageable and life's anxieties bearable, as stated by Siegel (1999) "that which is shareable is bearable". To be well connected is to be on the path of well-being and/or on the path to emotional and developmental healing.

The fields of developmental psychology and attachment, aided by the evolving discipline of interpersonal neurobiology, have opened the door to not only the critical importance of interpersonal connection, but also the nature of interactions supportive to that connection. In this text, I have attempted to provide some key guidelines for the use of the attachment model in work with children and adolescents whose behavior and needs have placed them in intensive treatment programs. At the core of my message has been a mandate for administrative support for training in relational connection and for clinical caretakers to intentionally employ an interactional style characterized by PACE (playfulness, acceptance, curiosity and empathy). This style, together with a deep commitment to repair relational tears when they occur, is the essence of this message.

As discussed in the Introduction, more and more children are receiving a larger percentage of their total care within institutional settings, both non-clinical (e.g. daycare, schools) and clinical (e.g. day treatment, hospitals). In light of this fact, it is imperative that our institutions learn to explicitly address and honor the critical importance of relational attachment, largely avoiding a distinction between the role and function of family vs. non-familial caretakers. If the institutions that are providing so much of our child care do not approach this work with wise, loving kindness, both our children and culture will undoubtedly suffer.

In a culture tossed about by rapid change, interpersonal impermanence and lives increasingly lived within social silos, the rising number of children and adolescents struggling to adapt and thrive must be seen as the "canaries in the mine," demanding an urgent and thoughtful approach to saving the miners, and hopefully even the vulnerable canaries. It is my hope that this text will help its readers take back to the institution in which they serve as caretakers the fundamental message: *Our kids need us, not simply as custodial caregivers but as mindful caregivers who proudly and fully love them.*

All kids, particularly our most vulnerable and troubled, desperately need us to support their growth and healing through relationships characterized by compassionate wisdom, patience and as uncomfortable as it may be to say for some of us within the clinical world – love.

REFERENCES

Baylin, J. and Hughes, D. (2016) *The Neurobiology of Attachment-Focused Therapy*. New York, NY: W.W. Norton.

Cozolino, L. (2013) *The Social Neuroscience of Education: Optimizing Attachment and Learning in the Classroom*. New York, NY: W.W. Norton.

Cozolino, L. (2014a) *Attachment-Based Teaching: Creating a Tribal Classroom*. New York, NY: W.W. Norton.

Cozolino, L. (2014b) *The Neuroscience of Human Relationships: Attachment and the Developing Social Brain*. New York: W.W. Norton.

Diamond, G. S., Diamond G. M. and Levy, S. (2014) *Attachment-Based Family Therapy for Depressed Adolescents*. Washington, DC, American Psychological Association.

Greene, R. and Ablon, J.S. (2006) *Treating Explosive Kids*. New York, NY: Guilford Press.

Greenspan, S. and Wieder, S. (2009) *Engaging Autism: Using the Floortime Approach to Help Children Relate, Communicate, and Think*. Lebanon, IN: Da Capo Books.

Gordon, M. (2005) *Roots of Empathy*. New York, NY: The Experiment.

Gutstein, S.E. and Sheely, R.K. (2002) *Relationship Development Intervention with Young Children: Social and Emotional Development Activities for Asperger Syndrome, Autism, PDD and NLD*. London: Jessica Kingsley Publishers.

Hughes, D.A. (2007) *Attachment-Focused Family Therapy*. New York, NY: W.W. Norton.

Hughes, D.A. (2009) *Attachment-Focused Parenting: Effective Strategies to Care for Children*. New York, NY: W.W. Norton.

Johnston, P.H. (2004) *Choice Words: How Our Language Affects Children's Learning*. Portland, ME: Stenhouse.

Kohut, H. (1971) *The Analysis of the Self*. New York, NY: International Universities Press.

Perry, B. and Szalavitz, M. (2006) *The Boy Who Was Raised as a Dog*. Philadelphia, PA: Basic Books.

Porges, S. (2011) *The Polyvagal Theory*. New York, NY and London: W.W. Norton.

Siegel, D. (2008) *The Neurobiology of We*. Audiobook. Louisville, CO: Sounds True.

Siegel, D. and Bryson, T.P. (2012) *The Whole Brain Child*. New York, NY: Bantam.

Siegel, D. and Bryson, T.P. (2014) *No Drama Discipline*. London: Scribe.

Siegel, D. and Hartzell, M. (2014) *Parenting from the Inside Out: How a Deeper Self-Understanding Can Help You Raise Children Who Thrive*. Brunswick, VIC: Scribe Publications.

Stern, D. (1985) *The Interpersonal World of the Infant*. New York, NY: Basic Books.

Stewart, J. (2002) *Beyond Time Out—A Practical Guide to Understanding and Serving Students with Behavioral Impairment in the Public Schools*. Portland, ME: HCA.

Szalavitz, M. and Perry, B. (2010) *Born for Love: Why Empathy Is Essential—and Endangered*. New York, NY: HarperCollins.

Residential Child Care Project (2010) *Therapeutic Crisis Intervention System: Information Bulletin.* Ithaca, NY: Bronfenbrenner Center for Translational Research, Cornell University.

Williams, M. (2017) *The Original Velveteen Rabbit.* London: Egmont UK.

Winnicott, D.W. (1953) 'Transitional objects and transitional phenomena: A study of the first 'not-me' possession.' *International Journal of Psycho-Analysis 34,* 2, 89–97.

Winnicott, D.W. (1958) *Through Pediatrics to Psychoanalysis.* New York, NY: Basic Books.

SUBJECT INDEX

AUTHOR INDEX

ABOUT THE AUTHOR

Dr. John Stewart is a psychologist, a senior child and family clinician and a respected clinical professor in the Tufts School of Medicine Department of Psychiatry. He has over 30 years of experience developing and supervising child and adolescent treatment programs within both clinical and educational settings. His clinical perspective is deeply attachment informed, yet pragmatic in its attunement to the need for consistency and structure. He has been a frequent presenter and consultant to child and adolescent programs across the country and is known for his clarity of thought, passion, warmth and humor. His life is split between Maine and Nicaragua where he lives with his wife with whom he shares two grown children, their spouses and three grandchildren.